OTHER BOOK  K

Facing Grief and Death
The Struggle For Meaning (editor)
Knowing God: Religious Knowledge in the Theology of John Baillie
Our Baptist Tradition
Ministry: An Ecumenical Challenge (editor)
Getting Past the Pain
A Glorious Vision
The Bible As Our Guide For Spiritual Growth (editor)
Authentic Evangelism
The Lord's Prayer Today
The Way for All Seasons
Through the Eyes of a Child
Christmas Is for the Young... Whatever Their Age
Love as a Way of Living
The Compelling Faces of Jesus
The Left Behind Fantasy
The Ten Commandments: Their Meaning Today
Facing Life's Ups and Downs
The Church In Today's World
The Church Under the Cross
Modern Shapers of Baptist Thought in America
The Journey to the Undiscovered Country: What's Beyond Death?
A Pastor Preaching: Toward a Theology of the Proclaimed Word
The Pulpit Ministry of the Pastors of River Road Church, Baptist
(editor)
The Last Words from the Cross
Lord, I Keep Getting a Busy Signal: Reaching for
a Better Spiritual Connection
Overcoming Sermon Block: The Preacher's Workshop
A Revolutionary Gospel: Salvation in the Theology of Walter
Rauschenbusch
Holidays, Holy Days, and Special Days: Preaching through the Year
Star Thrower: A Pastor's Handbook

PRAISE FOR *A POSITIVE WORD FOR CHRISTIAN LAMENTING*

William Tuck's *A Positive Word for Christian Lamenting* is an eminently practical work of pastoral theology, drawing on his years of preaching experience and pastoral service. I would especially recommend it for one who is new to pastoral ministry. Each "first funeral," for one late in life, for suicide or disease or accident or early in life, can be a frightening endeavor. This volume is filled with examples of funeral sermons for just such occasions. Reading it is like sitting with the author for personal consultation. The preface alone is worth purchasing the book! There are other books on the funeral as an industry and as a concept, but if the reader's questions is, "What do I say?" this is the place to find an answer.

Rev. Dr. David Moffett-Moore, Sr.
Pastor for Portage United Church of Christ, Portage MI, author of *The Jesus Manifesto: A Participatory Study Guide to the Sermon on the Mount* and *Wind and Whirlwind: Being a Pastor in a Storm of Change*

From years of rich pastoral experience comes a book of twenty-six homilies addressing a wide variety of losses including a difficult murder and suicide, the death of a child, a death at Christmas time, and the losses of his own mother and father. Tuck well exceeds his stated goal of assisting in the grieving process and celebrating life. His homilies are full of grace, creativity, and solid biblical exegesis. While many books on funerals offer good generic material, I have found none that speak to such a wide range of losses with such insight and sensitivity. This is a book not only for ministers but for all of those who would like to better understand their own grief and better understand how to stand with others who grieve. It is indeed a positive and most instructive word for Christian lamenting.

Dr. Ronald Higdon
Pastor Emeritus Broadway Baptist Church, Louisville, KY and author of *Surviving a Son's Suicide* and *In Changing Times: A Guide for Reflection and Celebration*

Everybody, sooner or later, will walk through the darkest valley – the valley of the shadow of death. And every pastor, sooner or later, will stand before family and friends to offer a message that incorporates aspects of the deceased's life and accentuates the Resurrection. Sometimes the pastor isn't sure how to say what needs to be said. I know first-hand. As a second-year seminary student serving a student pastorate I was informed of the completed suicide of a parishioner. Unsure of myself and how to approach the funeral I went to my preaching professor, Bill Tuck, who took the time to help me so I could be of help in that situation – especially the funeral. Now, more than 35 years later, my mentor – a seasoned author-pastor-preacher-teacher-theologian – presents a wonderful gift that offers exceptional insight on how to speak a word about the person and incorporate a faithful proclamation of the Gospel in the same setting. In *A Positive Word for Christian Lamenting*, Tuck provides 26 unique homilies addressing various situations and circumstances surrounding death. Not only is Tuck's work a must for pastors and professional care-givers, it is a good resource for anybody who has walked or is walking or will walk through the darkest valley. Sooner or later it will happen if it hasn't already. And Bill Tuck's book enables a mourner to engage a lament that is positively Christian.

Dr. Jimmy Gentry
Senior Pastor, Garden Lakes Baptist Church, Rome, GA

A POSITIVE WORD FOR CHRISTIAN LAMENTING

FUNERAL HOMILIES

WILLIAM POWELL TUCK

Energion Publications
Gonzalez, FL
2016

ISBN10: 1-63199-273-2
ISBN13: 978-1-63199-273-5
Library of Congress Control Number: 2016950335

Energion Publications
P. O. Box 841
Gonzalez, FL 32560

energion.com
pubs@energion.com

**Dedicated
to
the many families
to whom I have ministered
in their time of grief.**

TABLE OF CONTENTS

PREFACE

The death of a loved one is without question one of the most stressful and difficult times in any person's life. Comfort and support are essential for one to work through this time of grief. I believe that a properly conducted funeral service can assist in the grieving process. A funeral service affords the family an opportunity to reflect on the life of the deceased and receive the love and affirmation of family and friends during this season of grief. The service offers the family of the deceased an occasion and place to share their grief, feel the support and comfort of others, a public opportunity to say "good-bye" to their loved one and to hear the Christian affirmation of the assurance of life after death.

The homily delivered on this occasion provides the family a time to celebrate the life of the deceased loved one and to affirm the Christian hope of eternal life. The homily should not deny the harsh reality of pain, suffering, accidents or death but offer the family a reflective time to focus on the nature of the God of love in the midst of such sorrow. It should not offer easy answers to profound questions about suffering, pain and death but affirm that it is all right to ask questions, express anger or have lapses of doubts and anxiety. The homily should offer assurances that crying is normal and OK and not something which should muster feelings of shame or remorse. "Explanations, no matter how sincere," Friedrich Schleiermacher wrote, "rarely console." Suffering and grief will always have many unanswered questions. Every trial affords us an opportunity to learn new ways to respond to the mysteries of grief and pain and search deeper for the Presence of God in our grief and suffering. Above all, the homily is the chance to affirm the abiding presence of God in our grief and to express the Christian hope of life everlasting.

I always meet with the family sometime before the service and solicit words, stories and reflections about the deceased that I might use in the service. I allow them to suggest any scriptures, hymns or poems that might be appropriate for the service. I remind them that this is a service of worship and what we do in the service needs to be suitable for that context. I believe that the homily should make proper reference to the deceased, and I usually use some of the information I have heard from them when I talked with them before the service. A service without any personal reference to the loved one to me is inappropriate and not comforting to the family in their grief. The personal references should be focusing on the positive things in that person's life and is not a time to dwell on his or her weaknesses. Drawing on the biblical text for the homily, I seek to affirm the grace and love of God in Christ and the promise of life after death. I also do not attempt to make the service an evangelistic occasion, which I believe would be a mistake. I believe that those at the service can "overhear" the good news of the Gospel story in what is said that day. The homily should also be relatively brief and appropriate for the deceased and his or her family.

I normally read earlier in the service several selected biblical texts from the Old Testament and the New Testament such as Psalms 23, 46, 90,121, Isaiah 40:27-31, Proverbs 31:10-30, John 14:1-6, Romans 8:35-38, 1 Corinthians 15:42-44, 53-57, Revelation 21:4 and 22:4-5. I also include prayers such as an invocation and benediction as well as the Lord's Prayer at appropriate times in the order of the service. If any family member has a part in the service, I usually include her or him before the homily. Hymns, solos or choral music, if utilized, are also spaced in their appropriate order of the worship service. An Order of Worship is usually furnished to the worshippers so they can follow the service.

The following homilies are samples of funeral meditations I have preached over the years in various churches where I have served as pastor. The homilies reflect persons from various walks of life, different ages, some who died suddenly, and others who died after prolonged illnesses, suicides, etc. The names have been changed, but the homilies are a reflection of ministry to real people and an effort to meet genuine needs. None of these homilies is an attempt to produce "outstanding" sermons but are meditations that sought to offer comfort and hope to grieving families. There is always some repetition in funeral meditations since they all focus on some perspective of grief, suffering and the assurance of life after death. I also concluded many of my meditations with a poem or hymn, often using Tennyson's "Crossing the Bar" and Rudyard Kipling's "When Earth's Last Picture Is Painted." Even if I used one of these poems on several of the homilies included here, I decided to have them appear on only one of the meditations rather than being repeated several times.

Many of the psalms provide clear examples of laments to God. A least a third of the psalms are lament psalms, some forty-two are individual laments and sixteen are corporate laments. Lament examples can be found in Psalms 5, 6, 13, 22, 38, 44, 51, 77, 102, 103, 130 and others. Many view these psalms as negative and with an accusatory tone directed toward God. Some have questioned whether their tone is appropriate for Christian prayers. To me they reveal how persons have not only been completely honest in their prayers to God but have affirmed that God is open to all of our real feelings, and we do not have to play games with our deepest thoughts and anguish. Many people have often felt guilty if they have had negative, angry or hostile feelings toward God or others in their time of suffering or grief. But the laments in the Psalms reveal to us the openness of God to our deepest feeling whether they are positive or negative. We should also note that Jesus, deeply grieved and agitated, voiced his personal lament in the Garden of Gethsemane, "Father, if it is possible, let this cup pass from me" (Matthew 26:36-46) and on the cross with his agonizing cry, "My God, my God, why have you forsaken me?" (Mark 15: 34).

The homily in the funeral service should reflect a positive openness to the genuine feelings of those who are grieving without any stance of guilt or embarrassment. The minister has the opportunity to affirm the positive dimensions of lament and still offer the assurance of trust found in such Psalms as 4, 23, 73, 62, 100 and the New Testament words of hope. When people believe they can be honest with God, the minister and others, healing from their grief will occur sooner. Genuine lament can be a positive force in healing.

I want to express my appreciation again to my friend and fellow minister, Rand Forder, for his careful proofreading of the original manuscript.

1.

A Homily

for

Janice Gill
(A Teacher)

The Lord stood with me and strengthened me.
2 Timothy 4:17 (KJV)

Recently, our shores and the Gulf Coast have experienced great storms and hurricanes. A number of years ago in Tokyo, Japan, a devastating hurricane came through there and destroyed many of the houses. Two young girls went with their parents to their temple to pray. They said, "Our parents just looked up at the gods and scowled." But, she stated that Christians looked up to God, sang songs, prayed, and began to build their homes again.

Today, we acknowledge that this family has gone through many storms of suffering, pain, and death. During this time, they leaned back in quiet faith on God, and now you seek to begin to rebuild your lives. Paul reminds us, "The Lord stood with me and strengthened me." Today, we seek to acknowledge the God who stands with us and strengthens us.

CHRIST PRESENT IN JANICE'S LIFE

First, Christ stood with Janice Gill in her living. She was a teacher for twenty-five years. She taught English and Special Education. She had all the traits of a good teacher. She was caring, loving, patient, understanding, knowledgeable, and much more. Janice had a great compassion for children.

She and Dan shared thirty-five years of married life together. She was a good wife, a loving mother and loving grandmother. Her children said that she was, "My best friend." Even when they were far away across the country, they would call her on the phone and talk a lot. She was a great listener. She was patient, kind, compassionate, caring, and supportive of them no matter what. She was a loving mother who was always there for her children. She was the one who waited up late for them when they came home from a date when they were teenagers. Today, we honor her as a loving grandmother of her three grandchildren, and a loving mother of her three children.

The friends of Janice and Dan's children felt that she was a mother to them, as well. She took them in as her own when they would come to visit her children. They always felt welcomed and loved. She showed so much love for her children and their friends that, when their friends had moved away and would come back for a visit to Louisville, they would always come back and visit Janice in her home, as well.

We know that Janice took care of her mother during her mother's illness, off and on for three or four years while her mother was in her home. During Janice's illness, we know that Doris cared for Janice, as well. There was a loving relationship between Janice and her mother and father.

Several years ago, Karen gave her mother a little book of quotations and pictures that she had made for her. In it she has a poem entitled "Mother."

Mother, all my life you have given me your all;
It is time I share mine with you even if it is small.

I can never give you as much as you have given me;
But I will do my best, you will see.

Please forgive me when I was a young child,
I always took your love as if it was mild.

God gave me strength to love and to care;
It took twenty years to even take that dare.

It is you who has taught me this right.
It is you who I will thank every day, every night.

If you ever have a problem that you're unsure about,
Please let me know, God will give me
    the power to help you out.

CHRIST PRESENT IN ILLNESS AND DEATH

Second, Christ stood with Janice in her illness and death. For three years Janice struggled with cancer. During this time, she did not complain, but was patient with her family and those who waited upon her. Just as a small child walking with a parent in a fierce storm will lift up her hand into the hand of the parent for comfort and support, so Janice lifted up her hand in quiet trust into her Lord's hand. During the course of her illness, Janice had a strong spirit. She expressed on numerous occasions that she was not afraid of dying. She had a quiet trust and a strong faith. She said that she knew that, "The Lord is with me. I have an inner peace during this time." This inner peace came from the powerful presence of the spirit of Christ who stood with her and strengthened her.

Among Janice's Sunday School lesson notes and Bible, I found this poem which she had kept by Helen Steiner Rice; entitled "What More Can You Ask?" It affirms something of her faith and trust.

God's love endureth forever —
What a wonderful thing to know
When the tides of life run against you
And your spirit is downcast and low...

God's kindness is ever around you,
Always ready to freely impart
Strength to your faltering spirit,
Cheer to your lonely heart...

God's presence is ever beside you,
As near as the reach of your hand;
You have but to tell Him your troubles,
There is nothing He won't understand...

And knowing God's love is unfailing,
And His mercy unending and great,
You have but to trust His promise —
"God comes not too soon or too late" ...

So wait with a heart that is patient
For the goodness of God to prevail —
For never do prayers go unanswered,
And His mercy and love never fail.[1]

CHRIST CONTINUES TO OFFER STRENGTH

Third, Christ now stands with the family and friends to strengthen and support you today. You know that you are not alone. Christ is there with Dan, Dan Jr., Karen, and Layne. He is also with her mother, father, the three grandchildren, and the many friends. We know that life will be different now without Janice, but we know that she would want you to go on and live life to its fullest.

During this time, you have felt the support of your friends and church family through the meals, prayers, visits, and listening. You have felt the strength of God to guide and comfort you. God will continue to be there with you to support you. You know that you are not alone.

CHRIST OPENS THE DOOR TO LIFE BEYOND

Fourth, Christ stands with Janice now in her heavenly home. Janice leaned back in faith, and has gone to that place that Christ has prepared for her. Today, we affirm that death is not the end, but a beginning; death is not a dead-end, but a door that opens to a new and abundant life. Death is really a birthing from this life to the next life. We acknowledge that suffering and pain are real, but her suffering and pain are over. She now has a new spiritual body free of pain and suffering.

---

1   Helen Steiner Rice, "What More Can You Ask?" *Helen Steiner* Rice, *Just for Me* (Garden City, New York: Doubleday & Company, Inc., 1967), 38.

In the fall of the year, as the leaves drop off the trees, the trees seem to be bare. But, there are dormant buds on the trees which indicate life. Life continues to go on. And, in the springtime of the year, we will see the new life as it continues. God has built it into nature itself, and He has built it into our lives as well. Jesus said, "I am the resurrection and the life. Because I live, you will live also." We affirm our faith today, that Janice is now gone to that heavenly home that Christ has prepared for her.

A mother was walking with her daughter on the beach one day. They were talking about life and death. They found a shell of one of the departed sea creatures. The mother reached down, picked up the shell, and said to her daughter, "You see, this shell is now empty. The animal within it has departed, but it is still alive, still out there. One day we will come to the point where we will lay down our body. Our body is our shell, but the spirit, which is the true person, will continue to live on. We will leave our bodies and go to dwell in that eternal home that God has made for us. At some point our physical body will wear out. We will lay it aside and put on the spiritual body that God has given to each of us."

The family asked if I would share with you a poem entitled "The Legacy," which they feel presents some of their feelings and the love they had for Janice.

> When I die, give what is left of me to children.
> If you need to cry, cry for your brothers walking beside you.
> Put your arms around anyone and give them what you need to give me.
> I want to leave you something, something better than words or sounds.
> Look for me in the people I have known and loved.
> And if you cannot live without me, then let me live on in your eyes,
> your mind and your acts of kindness.
> You can love me most by letting hands touch hands
> and letting go of children that need to be free.
> Love does not die, people do.
> So when all that is left of me is love...
> Give me away ...
> (Author unknown)

Gracious God, as we come to this moment of saying good-bye to Janice, may we remember that You are here with us to strengthen us and hold us up. We pray Your blessings upon Dan, Dan Jr., Karen, and Lucy. May they feel the continuous embrace of Your love as they walk through the valley of the shadow of death. Open their eyes to the abundant life, and life everlasting which we have through Christ, our Lord. May they lean upon You for strength and help, and have the assurance that death is not the end, but the beginning of a new and abundant life. Through Christ, our Lord, we pray. Amen.

2.

A Homily
for
Myrtle Bates
(A Lengthy Illness)

"Through the Shadows"

Psalm 23

The Twenty-Third Psalm is the favorite of many people. This is indeed a wonderful Psalm. Phillips Brooks, one of the great ministers in America years ago, described this Psalm as "the nightingale of the Psalms." He ascribed it as such because the nightingale sings its sweetest when the night is darkest. As a family you have come to the dark moment of grief because your loved one, Myrtle Bates, has died. The shock and grief of her death have forced family and friends to walk through the shadows of the valley of death.

THE LORD IS MY SHEPHERD

The Twenty-Third Psalm, however, offers us great help and support. It begins with a strong affirmation, "The Lord is my shepherd." You and I come to the valley of the shadow of death aware that we do not face death alone, but we have the strength and presence of God to go with us through that valley. We place our hands and our troubled hearts in God's hands. We have the assurance that God is present with us, to walk beside us and strengthen us to face the burden of grief that lies before us. Just as the shepherd cared for the sheep in ancient times and modern places today, Christ, as our Good Shepherd, walks beside us with love and peace.

A PLACE OF REST AND GUIDANCE

The Psalm says: "The Lord makes me lie down." We find in this moment of grief our rest, peace and refuge in the presence of God who is here with us. "He leads me." God gives us guidance and a sense of direction. The shock of grief leaves us puzzled and confused and we are not sure we can feel God's presence. But we have to remember that God's presence is not based on feelings. Sometimes we are low because of our grief and God is ever present to guide us, strengthen us and walk with us into the days that lie before us.

GOD'S RENEWAL

The Psalm says: "He restores my soul." You need to look to God to find renewal, reinvigoration and strength to help bear you up.

A small boy was struggling one day with a heavy log, trying to bring it to his father to be used in the fireplace. Finally, he stumbled and dropped the log.

The father said, to the young son, "Why didn't you use all of your strength?"

The small boy, a bit hurt, said, "But Dad, I did."

"No! No! you didn't," the father said, "You did not ask me to help you."

This is the great truth of the Psalm. God is with us. We can't bear this grief alone, but God is present to help you. God is with you. God offers companionship, a sense of His presence. We know that we are never alone.

WALKING THROUGH THE VALLEY

The Psalm says, "Yea, though I walk through the valley." The Bible often uses "walking' as a word to describe the different aspects of life. In Genesis it states: "Before whom my fathers did walk" (Genesis 48:15). "Ask the good way and walk therein" (Jeremiah 6:18). Micah reminds us, "Walk humbly with your God" (Micah 6:8). "Walk in newness of life" (Romans 6:4). "Walk worthy of your vocation" (Ephesians 4: 1). "Walk worthy of the Lord" (Colossians 1:9).

We pause today to remember the walk of Myrtle Bates. For 85 years she walked the good life among us. She experienced, like all of us, good times and difficult times, happy and sad moments, joys and sorrows. But through it all, she was a good woman. We thank God for her life. Today we express our gratitude for the years we shared with her as family and friends. But, even at its longest, life is still brief. We know life will be different without her and she will be missed but we are thankful for the many years that she walked among us. Today she is survived by two sons, seven grandchildren, and six great grandchildren.

We observed her walk and the way she lived. Myrtle was faithful in her church attendance until she became older and ill. For 20 years she was a Nursing Associate. She enjoyed this work and was good at it. She worked with Southeastern General Hospital until she was 72. She was good hearted to strangers and enjoyed being with older people. She admired her mother and talked about her a great deal. She was serious minded and devoted to Wilton. She was a good woman of religious faith. Myrtle's influence will continue to be felt by family and friends through many years to come.

THE VALLEY OF SHADOWS

In Palestine there is a valley known as "The Shadow of Death." It is a frightening place for sheep and for people. It is a fierce place with steep slopes and rugged terrain. Often, in Biblical days, there were robbers waiting to pounce on people who came through there or to steal the sheep. This valley of the shadows is indeed frightening. Look for a moment at this valley of the shadows. Shadows often hide and distort reality. The pathway through grief may look dark and gloomy as it did through the Shadow of Death Valley. But we have to remember the emphasis is on the word *through*. We pass through those shadows which distort the reality which is before us.

Remember that the shadows themselves have no reality. A shadow is not real. Remember, wherever you have a shadow, there is light shining behind it because there can be no shadow without light. The shadow is the resultant gloom caused by something between you and the light. Remember that the shadows vanish when you face the light. If we stay in the shadows of grief, we will feel low. When we walk toward the light, then the shadows will disappear. They fall behind us. Let us turn and look toward the light of God's presence which shines in our face to remind us that death is not the end. The key emphasis, I think, in this line is "Yea, though I walk *through* the valley of the shadow of death, I will fear no evil." We walk ***through*** the valley of the shadow of grief today assured that death is not the end. Myrtle has gone to be with the God she loves. The shadows of grief are for a moment. We need to remember that the light of God's love shines on behind us and we have the assurance that death is not the end.

Years ago when I was in school, I remember preaching in a small mountain church. I got there and it was night, and in the winter months, it was dark and dreary. As I pulled up in my little Ford before that church, it seemed dark, lonesome and dreary. As I walked toward the church, I thought this is, indeed, going to be a depressing service. I assumed since I saw no light that there would not be many present for the service. But when I opened the door, light flooded out toward me from the church that was filled with many lights and filled with people who had gathered there to worship.

On this side of death, it may look gloomy and sad to us, but when the door of death is opened, light floods into our lives and the shadows disappear. The light of God's presence sustains us and we walk into the eternal life that God has prepared. Myrtle has gone to that land of light. She no longer is in the land of shadows. She has found the peace of God. May God come into our lives to give us a sense of peace and rest and may we find comfort in knowing that for her, she has gone from this life to dwell in the eternal realm that God has prepared.

Alfred Lord Tennyson has expressed his faith in life beyond death in these beautiful lines in his "In Memoriam."

Strong Son of God, Immortal Love,
Whom we, that have not seen thy face,
By faith, and faith alone, embrace,
Believing where we cannot prove;

Thou wilt not leave us in the dust:
Thou madest man, he knows not why,
He thinks he was made not to die;
And thou hast made him: thou art just.

We have but faith; we cannot know;
For knowledge is of things we see;
And yet we trust it comes from thee,
A beam in darkness; let it grow.

Let knowledge grow from more to more,
But more of reverence in us dwell;
That mind and soul, according well,
May make one music as before,
But vaster.[2]

   *O God of Light, we come to this moment of death, express-
ing our grief at the loss of this good woman, Myrtle Bates. We
thank you for her life among us, for her faith and hope. Encircle the family now in the arms of Your love and give them the
assurance that death is not the end. May they know that truly
we walk through valley into the land of eternal life that you
have prepared. May Your comfort, peace, love and grace abide
in the hearts of the family both now and forevermore. Amen.*

---

2   Alfred Lord Tennyson, "In Memoriam," James Dalton Morrison, editor.
     Masterpieces of Religious Verse (New York: Harper & Brothers Publishing,
     1948), 327-328.

A Homily

for

Phyllis Cave and Brandon Shaw
(Murder and Suicide)

Romans 8:18-27

A t a time like this, words cannot adequately express all that we feel or would like to say. When death intrudes our life suddenly and as unexpectedly as the events over the past few days did, we are overwhelmed with emotion, anger and many unresolved questions. Nevertheless, we gather this afternoon to share our grief but more to probe the mystery of such a tragedy and to try and sense the presence of God.

WE STAND BEFORE THE MYSTERY OF DEATH AND SEARCH FOR LIGHT.

We come today first of all acknowledging the mystery of life. For all of us there is a sense of shock and denial, some sense of depression, physical symptoms, and even some hostility. Questions run through our minds. Why is there such suffering and pain? Why does God allow such tragedies to happen? These are your questions and my questions. We acknowledge that we cannot understand all of the mystery of life. Suffering and death have no easy word. There is no right word for such a time as this.

But death is not the only mystery of life. So is birth itself. So is the beauty of fall, the coldness of winter, the budding of life in the spring, and the warmth of summer. There is a mystery also in birth and growing, in loving and caring. We can't understand it all. The buds on the trees in the springtime of the year remind us that life goes on. They have been dormant all through winter, but the warmth of spring brings them back to life. Flowers blossom forth from the seeds and bulbs that have been planted so that we have their loveliness in the summer. No one can explain so easily how life continues or why it ends as it does. There is a deep sense of mystery.

THANKFUL FOR THE GIFT OF LIFE

We also thank God for the gift of life. We thank God for the years shared with Phyllis and Brandon. Family members remember Phyllis when she had a full head of brown curly hair. Family members loved to call her "Baby doll." When she was young, she loved life, was energetic, filled with laughter, fun-loving and loved to tease her brother and others. She was a caring and affectionate person. She has always been good and faithful to her closest friends. She enjoyed fishing and camping with her family when she was young. She loved her family dearly. As she got older, she seemed to develop a low sense of self-esteem. Although gifted and intelligent, she struggled with her own self-direction in life. One of her songs entitled "Vapors" expresses something of this feeling. Listen to her words and the poetry that she wrote:

> Vaporized beam that I am, no more in time,
> than a shift of sand.
> In a world that's not mine.
> I know that I'm
> passin' through
> with one secret of life.
> It's all in your mood.

> Take stride in your strife. Hey, live your life.
> Vaporized beam that I am, no more in time,
> than a shift of sand.
> In a world that's not mine.

> Vaporized beam that I am,
> travelling this land.
> Let me always be kind,
> to that other man in time.
> Vaporized beam that I am, no more in time,
> than a shift of sand.
> In a world that's not mine.

She did not seem to have enough self-confidence in herself. For some time now, Phyllis became obsessed that someone was going to harm Brandon and her. In her confused emotional state,

Phyllis thought that her tragic act would somehow protect them from a greater danger. She loved Brandon deeply, and in her mental sickness she thought she was protecting him. We can never fully get inside her mind but we all know that she wanted most of all to protect Brandon. We know she did not respond in a rational way as you and I see it. She was ill and acted out of her illness.

Brandon was a handsome, warm, affectionate, generous young man. He had lots of friends and loved to be with hem. He was gifted and loved to make things. He loved to put things together. He enjoyed building, especially driving nails. Sometimes he would drive them in trees in the back yard. He was proud recently of getting an 'A' in conduct. He loved to play with trains and had several sets. He loved his grandparents and they loved him and cared for him deeply. Clarence recalls just recently Brandon running up behind him and hugging him and asking, "Are you my buddy?" Rose heard his prayers each night and in his own sweet way he offered his prayers for his family and friends. I remember him coming out of church and he would always hug my leg before he left.

Phyllis' problems drove her inward, but she did turn more to her faith and reached out to God in these last days. One of her poems reflects this quest. It is entitled "Pure Rain."

> All I've got
> Is this song for you, world.
> With all the pain and suffering you've endured.
>   Can not peace and pain blend in the rain?
> So that God's World will not be stained.
>
> Can the people's blood, sweat and labor make a difference?
> Or will it, all be in vain?
> Surely to God,
> in the end.
>
> All the suffering will blend in the rain.
> Countries forever warring.

Jealousy, Hate and Greed.
In the end, all they
will have achieved,
is blood and suffering in the rain.

Can the people come to peace?
Swallow their hate and pride.
Cannot man learn to love,
and set war and anger aside?

C'mon people, I know there must be a way,
come to terms,
and forget the pain,
and put peace and love,
in pure rain.

We will miss them. Life will not be the same. But just as the sun leaves an afterglow when it sets in the west, so Phyllis and Brandon left an afterglow from their lives that will remain in our heart and memory.

THE GOODNESS OF GOD

And we continue to affirm the goodness of God, even in the face of death. We reaffirm our faith today in the goodness of God and rest on the conviction that his love is eternal and strong. God created life out of his love and he sustains it. We do not know why God has created the possibility of tragedies like this happening. They are a part of the universe God has created. Without the possibility of suffering and pain, there could be no growth or maturing. We know that God does not deliberately send these things upon us. Today, like a small child, we place our hand in the hand of God to lean upon him for trust and strength. We know our strength is not enough.

THE VALLEY OF GRIEF

Next, we know, and won't forget, that family and friends are walking through a dark valley of grief. But we come to this valley of grief armed with the assurance that God is present with us. A favorite writer of mine, Harry Emerson Fosdick, who went through a deeply personal tragic experience, wrote once: "It was the most terrifying wilderness I ever traveled through. I dreadfully wanted to commit suicide. But instead I made one of the most vital discoveries in my life, I found God in a desert." Sometimes our deepest insights are discovered in the valley. We find that in the midst of despair, pain, and suffering that God is there. Even when we do not know it or feel it, He is there. We grieve but we grieve not as those who have no hope. We grieve with a sense of trust in the presence of God who is with us. Phyllis expresses something of her trust in the poem entitled, "Miracle Man."

> Did you walk across the water, Lord? Just to prove to me.
> That you can always be there, in my hour of need.
> Did you multiply the loaves of bread? Just so man might see.
> That if all we wait patiently, some miracle might be.
> Did you heal that man with leprosy? Just to show us all,
> that there is a larger plan.
> We should follow or we'll fall.
> Did you tire Lord of Miracles? Just to prove to man.
> That you were the Son of God, who gives life upon this land.
> Did you walk across the water, Lord? Just to prove to me.
> That you can always be there, in my hour of need.

WE WEEP WITH HOPE

We weep today, but we weep not as those who have no hope. We acknowledge that it is all right to cry. It is OK to acknowledge that we have sorrow at Phyllis and Brandon's death, but we do not grieve as those who have no hope. Death and the grave are not the end for the Christian. Jesus himself wept beside the grave of his friend Lazarus, and so we know it is good to express our grief and not to keep it deep down inside of us. We acknowledge that we grieve because life will be different without them. But we shall be able to face life and go on, because we have the presence of God with us. We acknowledge that although they are no longer with us, they are present with God where there is no suffering or pain. Our God's love is unconditional and knows the whys of such acts far better than we and forgives all. God knew Phyllis' detached state and forgives her.

PEACE OF CHRIST

We come also to thank God today for the assurance of peace which we have from Christ. Today we rest on the promise of life eternal through Christ. Our great sorrow is to be separated from Phyllis and Brandon, but we have the assurance today that through the grace of God they dwell in that marvelous eternal realm with him. As we lean upon God in faith, we know that one day we shall join them in the eternal realm where there is no hurt or sorrow but only peace.

DEATH AS A NEW BEGINNING

Last, we thank God that death is not the end but a new beginning. The flowers present today are a sign of the love and devotion of friends and family. But they also symbolize for us the resurrection garden on Easter Day when Jesus Christ himself rose from the grave. They give to us an assurance that death is not the end but a doorway that opens from this life to a new life, where the spiritual person is with God. Jesus said, "I have gone to prepare a place for you." He has gone to prepare that place for Phyllis and Brandon. They are there with God where they will dwell eternally in the home which he has made. We, of course, shall miss them, but today we rest with the assurance that they are with Christ and dwell eternally with him without pain and suffering. Each of us one day shall join them. Jesus said, "Because I live, you shall live also."

Look to the butterfly for a lesson on the transformation of life. For awhile the life of the humble caterpillar is restricted to crawling on a green leaf on a tree in the woods. All it knows of life is limited to that world. But one day, some stirrings within cause the caterpillar to enter a cocoon, and shortly it emerges, transformed into a beautiful, elegant butterfly with wings. It is no longer limited to the territory of the green leaf but can soar above the trees and world around it. Like the caterpillar, death takes us through a process of transformation where we are no longer limited by our earthy existence but enter into a new creation into the heavenly home which God has prepared for us. Death is a birthing from our earthly life into our spiritual existence.

It is a birthing from this life to the spiritual life. There we meet God, our loving Father, who awaits us to give us a new and abundant life that is beyond our imagination. Death is a birthing from this life to the eternal life. Today we affirm our hope and assurance in life everlasting. For us as Christians, death is a birth from this world to the next. May God give us the sense to know that his presence and assurance are with us today and in the weeks ahead.

> *Eternal Father, bind up the broken hearts today with the balm of your presence. Draw Clarence, Rose, John, and Guy and other family members and friends close to yourself and may they sense your shepherding care and presence in the days ahead. May the memories of the good life with Phyllis and Brandon and the assurance of life everlasting give to each of us in this hour comfort and assurance. Through Christ we pray. Amen.*

4.

A Homily
for
Lola Harvey
(A Heart Condition)

Easter Season

The Lord gave and the Lord has taken away. Blessed be the name
of the Lord.
Job 1:21 (NRSV)

This morning we have gathered to pay tribute to a departed loved one, Lola Harvey. We have gathered to express our grief and to sense the supportive, loving presence of God. We acknowledge our sadness but celebrate the gift of her life. We acknowledge that our grief and pain are real, but we also affirm our faith and hope in life everlasting and in the goodness of God. Job wrote, centuries ago, "The Lord gave and the Lord has taken away. Blessed be the name of the Lord" (Job 1:21). Let's see if we can draw some comfort from this text.

The Lord Gave/Gift

All life is a gift. We acknowledge that everything that we have comes to us as a gift from God. God is a loving creator. God has given us life as the most wondrous gift. We pause today to thank God for the years that we have shared with Lola, for the joys, hopes and blessings. We know that she loved life and rejoiced in it. But life is always brief, even at its longest and to see Lola's candle extinguish so quickly has been difficult.

The Gift of Happiness

Family and friends focus today upon the many years of happiness they shared with Lola. Friends and family spoke about her sense of serenity, peace, and contentment. She was a strong person, but a giving person who was always reaching out to others. She expressed her gift of life through love. She was a loving wife. She and Wilson shared sixty-six years of marriage together. She was not only his wife but soul mate and best friend. There was an absolute trust between them. She was a supportive and a loving wife in the finest sense of that word.

She was also a loving mother. She made her home a place where not only her children felt comfortable and loved but so did their friends. It was a place their friends wanted to come after school and games. She was always there for her family. She took care of them with love and devotion. Her grandchildren were a great delight in her life. She loved them and expressed it in so many ways.

Lola was also a caring person. Those who knew her well always saw her as a tender person, concerned for others and their problems. She was also always doing for others. She was completely unselfish and supportive of all of her family. Her sisters said she had been like a second mother to them. She was a great influence on all of her family. Her sisters said she may have been the smallest in size but she was the biggest in influence.

She welcomed everybody into her home. She was always willing to stretch out her hand and her food at mealtimes to include others. She loved her church and was always there for Sunday School, worship and on Wednesday night. You knew how supportive she was of her church by her faithfulness in attendance. She lived her faith by her action and faithfulness.

In one of Lola's devotional books she had included a leaflet entitled "Life's Little Instructions." Let me read some selections from that which are certainly symbolic of her attitude toward life and which I think greatly influenced her:
"Compliment three people everyday."
"Watch a sunrise once a year."
"Treat everyone you meet as you want to be treated."
"Never waste an opportunity to tell someone you love them."
"Become the most positive, enthusiastic person you know."
"Be forgiving of yourself and others."
"Say thank you a lot."
"Rekindle old friendships."
"Be the first to say hello."
"Make new friends but cherish the old ones."
"Be there when people need you."
"Never underestimate the power of love."
"Start and end each day with a prayer."

These words are instructive of Lola's philosophy of life and exemplify her attitude toward others.

We also celebrate the gift today of God's salvation. Paul says, "Thanks be to God for his unspeakable gift." One of Lola's favorite passages was John 3:16, "For God so loved the world that he gave his only begotten son that whosoever believes in him should not perish but have everlasting life." Today we are sure that Lola shares in this eternal life because of her deep faith in God. In her own very quiet personal way, she committed her hands in absolute faith and trust to God.

THE LORD TAKES AWAY / GRIEF

The writer of Ecclesiastes reminds us that for everything there is a season, a time to be born and a time to die, a time to laugh and a time to cry. Job knew that, just as God gave the gift of life, so suffering and death were also a part of life. Today we acknowledge that life is filled with seasons that come and go. We are now passing through the season of winter with its coldness, damp rain and freezing weather. We are on the dawning of springtime. We have already seen buds breaking forth on trees, flowers pushing up toward the sun and grass beginning to turn green. The warmth of springtime is upon us. Soon the seasons will move on. There will be the heat of summer and then, later the dazzling colors of fall. Seasons come and change and move on. They are a part of the mystery of life. Birth and death, laughter and pain, joy and grief, are also a part of life

PAIN AND SUFFERING

For many of us today there is a sense of shock that this good woman has slipped away so quickly. We acknowledge that we can not understand all of the mystery of life or death. Suffering and death have no easy word. There is not just one right word for such a time as this. Nevertheless, we continue to affirm our faith in the goodness of God even in the face of death. We will rest upon the conviction that God's love is eternal and strong. God created life out of his love and God sustains life. I do not know why God has created the possibilities of heart trouble and cancer. They are part of the universe God has created. Without the possibilities of suffering and pain, there could be no possibility of growth or maturity. We do know, however, that God does not deliberately send suffering and pain and grief upon us but like a small child we place our hand in the hand of God and lean upon God with trust and strength.

Lola acknowledged her trust of God as she faced her surgery. I spoke with her on the Thursday before her surgery and sensed her fears and yet also her strong faith. Her faith enabled her to know that God was there with her. She leaned back upon God and trusted that his way was good, even if she did not get well.

We acknowledge that death is real and our grief is real. We know that it is okay to cry. Jesus stood by the grave of Lazarus, his friend, and he too, wept. Crying is a normal part of our grief and God understands our sorrow. But we do not weep as those who have no hope. We weep in the assurance that the grave is not the end, but there is life beyond death.

We know that God and friends today are walking through the dark valley of grief. We come to this valley of grief however, armed with the assurance that God is present with us. Sometimes in our deepest valleys we are able to find the presence of God. In the midst of our despair, pain and suffering, God is ever present. God has promised us in Romans 8, that nothing separates us from his presence. We grieve, but we grieve with a sense of trust in the presence of God, who is there with us in this wilderness place.

BLESSED BE THE NAME OF THE LORD/ GLORY

We affirm that physical life is not the end. Lola had a strong faith in God and we rest in confidence today that God has prepared a place for her. Lola often opened her home to other people and welcomed them. This reminds me of Mary and Martha and how they opened their home to Jesus. It was in the home of friends like this that Jesus said the word, "I am the resurrection and the life." The words of Jesus assure us that death is a passageway from this life to the next. Death is not a dead-end but it is a birthing from this world to the next world. Death opens a door from the physical world to the eternal world.

Lola trusted God and put her hand in God's hand. In quiet faith she leaned back and trusted in God. Just as a small child in a dark room reaches out to hold the hand of his mother or father, so today we know that Lola has reached out her hand in the dark valley and grasped the hand of Jesus, our Lord, who has led her through this valley to life eternal.

When a person moves from one city to another we encourage them to transfer their letter to another church. Today, Lola has transferred her letter from the church mortal to the church eternal, from First Baptist Church to God's eternal home. We recommend her to God with great joy. We know that Lola's good influence will continue. Her influence will not be concluded with her death. She may no longer be with us and we know that the joy and happiness she brought will be missed. Nevertheless, she will be long remembered. In a Dennis the Menace cartoon, Dennis is playing on the floor with a toy truck and looks up at his father as his mother leaves the room and says, "Did you ever notice that Mom's smile stays here even when she is gone?"

That will also be true with Lola. The impact of her smile, unselfish attitude, service, love and devotion will continue to be felt long after she is gone. Her influence for good, joy and radiance will leave an afterglow among us. Life will be different without her but her influence will still be felt.

Just as Jesus assured Mary at the grave of Lazarus that he was the resurrection and the life, today we trust this same Christ in faith and affirm that death is a birthing from this life to the life beyond where there is eternal life. In this Easter season, we celebrate the resurrection of Jesus Christ. The apostle Paul reminds about the truth of the resurrection. He affirms that what is sown is perishable, what is raised is imperishable. It is sown in dishonor but it is raised in glory. It is sown a physical body and it is raised a spiritual body. Death is swallowed up in victory. Thanks be to God for the victory he gives us through our Lord, Jesus Christ.

Eternal Father, bind up the broken hearts today with the balm of your presence. Draw William, Carl, Sally, the grandchildren, great-grandchildren, sisters and other family members and friends close to yourself. May they sense your shepherding care and presence in the days ahead. May the memories of the good life with Lola and the assurance of life everlasting give to each of us in this hour comfort and courage. Amen.

A Homily

for

Peter H. Shane, Jr.
(Suffered with influenza)

Romans 8:35-39

Today we have gathered to see if we cannot capture a sense of comfort and assurance of God's grace as we reflect on some memories and positive thoughts about Pete Shane. This will, of course, not be the whole story of his life but a quick glance. We acknowledge our grief, yet reach for the comfort of God.

We Celebrate the Gift of Life

Let us begin by affirming the goodness of life. We remember today the good times and difficult times in Pete's life. We remember the

Happy moments and sad times,
Victories and defeats,
Joys and sorrows,
Health and sickness,

Peace and struggles.

We acknowledge that these are all a part of life.

Life comes to us as a wonderful gift. Pete tried to live his life to the fullest. He did not blame God for his own illness and suffering. He had suffered with influenza for eight years. He recognized this disease simply as a part of life, a difficult part. God gives us the gift of life. What we make of this life is our gift to God. Today we affirm Pete's good life.

He was an independent thinker. He prided himself on walking to a different beat. He had these words by Thoreau over his telephone. "If a man does not keep pace with his companions, perhaps it is because he hears the beat of a different drummer." Pete was true to his own beliefs. He was true to his own convictions. He was not always concerned with whether others agreed with him or not. He was a free thinker. What someone else was thinking did not necessarily float his boat. He would often turn his boat and move against the stream. He was a Type A personality, wired, and had difficulty relaxing. He liked to work, and he worked hard.

WALKING HIS OWN WAY

Pete worked hard in the family business, the Lumberton Family Linen Supply Service. He was devoted to his family and gave himself to his business. He said once to Nell, "I am not a lawn man, I am a laundry man." He grew up in the laundry. He spent over sixty years in that business. He was a hard worker and was dedicated to his task and goal. He used to make scale models of his equipment before he would purchase what he would actually need in his laundry.

Pete was a person who thought things through carefully. He pondered things for a long time. He looked to see the result. He was a focused person. He did not see shades of gray. He saw everything often in his own way and liked to do that one thing at a time. Pete was extremely bright. He loved to read, especially military history. General Patton and General McArthur were his heroes. He admired their military strategy and tactics. He recognized the importance of discipline and commitment to a purpose. His love of the military and strong patriotism came from his years at Edwards Military Institute. At his graduation, he was elected best drill cadet. In his freshman year at Clemson, he was elected the best drill cadet. His years in the Navy in World War II increased his love of the military.

He shared with me one of his favorite stories about General Patton. Patton had tried to move his army at the Battle of the Bulge, but wet weather had made it impossible. General Patton went into a small church and prayed for God to stop the rain and provide a way. The next morning the ground was frozen solid and Patton was able to move his men and equipment. They won the battle. Later in that same small church, General Patton prayed to God and thanked him for the victory and then added, "I would never have thought about the frozen ground. You are a (expletive deleted) good military strategist, Sir."

Pete was extremely bright. He was a person of the highest integrity, honesty, and strong character in business and life. Pete and Nell were married for forty-five years. They have three sons and two grandsons. Gerry said that Pete taught him everything he knew about the laundry business and encouraged him to learn the things that he had never learned. No one could have given her husband any better care than Nancy did during Pete's illness.

A CREATIVE PERSON

Pete was an artist. His artistic side was strong. He loved music and drama. He was active in the Little Theater but not as an actor on the stage. He worked behind the scenes making the sets for the background. He was not an out front person. In an obituary article about an actor, the paper noted that the actor never played any major roles but was invaluable in minor parts. Pete served in the background and had invaluable roles.

Pete liked to work with wood, furniture and carving. He liked what he could do with wood. He liked to paint, especially oil painting. There is a self portrait which looks like a van Gogh. He took his children one time to an art museum in Washington, D.C. He asked them to look at the impressionist paintings first by going up close to the front of the painting, and then stepping back and seeing what a difference each perspective made. He constructed a model of a PT boat which was like the 177 he was on in World War II. Though Pete had a creative side, he was also a bottom line person. He would quickly give you the essence of something. But he was a good friend who would be there for you. But even his gun was unconventional, a 351.

He liked the poetry of Robert Frost. The following poem, "The Road Not Taken," reflects Pete's perspective on life.

> Two roads diverged in a yellow wood,
> And sorry I could not travel both
> And be one traveler, long I stood
> And looked down one as far as I could

To where it bent in the undergrowth;
Then took the other, as just as fair,
And having perhaps the better claim,
Because it was grassy and wanted wear;
Though as for that the passing there
Had worn them really about the same,
And both that morning equally lay
In leaves no step had trodden black.
Oh, I kept the first for another day!
Yet knowing how way leads on to way,
I doubted if I should ever come back.
I shall be telling this with a sigh
Somewhere ages and ages hence:
Two roads diverged in a wood, and I –
   I took the one less traveled by,
And that has made all the difference.[3]

A QUESTIONING FAITH

Pete had a faith like Thomas. Thomas is one of my favorite disciples. Tennyson wrote, "There lives more faith in honest doubt; believe me, than half the creeds." Like Thomas, the disciple, Pete would not accept easy answers or cliches about religion. He was not one to walk in step with everyone else's religion. He was not a pack thinker. He felt free to ask questions. He would seek the truth from different sources. Pete was not impressed by verbiage, glitz or appearance. He was often turned away from church by those who said they were religious but he saw their hypocrisy. He had great difficulty with that failing. He could see through sham and show and demanded integrity in religion as well as in the rest of life. He felt he was not good enough. Like Thomas, Pete was not easily convinced about anything. He needed evidence and proof. He wanted real data, prudential evidence, and somebody else to prove it first. He pondered religious questions and beliefs a long time.

---

3   Robert Frost, "The Road Not Taken," *The Road Not Taken: A Selection of Robert Frost's Poems* (New York: Henry Holt & Company, 1971), 270.

Our Lord does not blame a person for wanting to know and for asking questions. Pete and I talked at great length. He expressed his belief in God and God's love of him. He did not fold over at the end and simply parrot phases that persons wanted him to say. He could not really do that. We had several conversations about church, God, life and death. I am convinced that his trust in God was real. He leaned back in his faith on God quietly. He said he wished that we had met twenty years ago. I assured him that it was OK to raise questions and have doubts about God. There were things about God and death which he simply did not know. And neither do I. I am always uncomfortable with those persons who are so sure about the temperature of hell and the furniture of heaven. Our knowledge of the life beyond this one is limited by the images and pictures we have in the Scriptures. And these are few.

Pete was not angry, but baffled, confused and concerned. He had the right to raise questions. I think faith is a footbridge that we really do not know whether it will hold us up over the chasm until we are forced to walk out on to it. When Pete was up against the end, he knew that God was in his life. He affirmed the unconditional love of God. He died as he had lived with questions and no easy answers. He carried a quote in his billfold from Jean De La Fontaine, "By the work, one knows the workman." His life was a reflection of the man of integrity he was.

Trust in God.

God's love is unconditional. Pete had questions until the end. He had fears about death like we all have. One time he asked me to stay with him when he was having difficulty breathing and Nell and others were not there. I remained until he could breathe easier. I was glad he felt he could ask. He struggled for eight years with breathing problems. Wednesday when I saw him, he was not able to talk. He probably had had a stroke. But he was still able to nod. I reminded him about God's love and asked him to remember that he was not separated from God's love. I reminded him that I knew he loved God, as we had talked before. He and I had talked on several occasions about death and what life was like beyond this life. I had no easy answers for him but words I had read from Christ who taught us to trust God who created us and loved us. The next day, he leaned back in quiet trust and died peacefully.

I shared with him one day a story from John Baillie, the Scottish theologian, about a man who went to see a dying friend. They were talking about death and what was beyond, when they heard a scratching at the door. "Do you hear that scratching at the door?" the man asked. "That's my dog. He has never been inside your house, but he knows his master is here and that is enough." We do not have all the answers about life beyond death. But we know that God is there. And that is enough. God is good and God's love is unconditional. And that is enough.

Loving God, comfort us now with your presence, and may we leave this place with the assurance of your unconditional grace and life everlasting. Amen.

6.

A Homily

for

Kathleen Harris
(A Cancer Patient and Faithful Christian)

Job 1:21

This morning we have gathered to pay tribute to a departed loved one, Kathleen Harris. We have gathered to express our grief and to sense the presence of God. We acknowledge our sadness but celebrate the gift of her life. We acknowledge that grief and pain are real but so also are our faith and hope.

Job said "The Lord gave and the Lord has taken away. Blessed be the name of the Lord" (Job 1:21).

THE LORD GAVE – LIFE AS A GIFT

All life is a gift. We acknowledge that everything we have comes to us as a gift from God. God is the Creator; he has given us life. We thank God for the years shared with Kathleen, for the joys, hopes and blessings. We know that she loved life and rejoiced in it. But life is always brief even at it longest.

THE GIFT OF HAPPINESS.

We recall many hours of happiness with Kathleen. She had the ability to make others happy. There was a glow and joy in her life. She was a beautiful and vibrant person. She was someone whom others enjoyed being with. Others spoke of her sense of humor, happiness and contentment. She enjoyed life. She was a strong person, a giving person who reached out to others. She liked to pick out the good qualities in others; rather than looking for the worst, she would look for the best in other people.

THE GIFT OF SERVICE

We acknowledge her gift of service. She was retired Director of Jefferson County Department of Public School Food Service, President of Kentucky Food Service, and former President of Jefferson County Public School Food Service Assistance. I read through a scrapbook which contained many letters written to her on her retirement. They all stated how much she had meant to the school system. She always wanted to see that children got a good meal at school. Her expertise in this area got her many awards and recognitions for her hard work. She had a citation entitled "Angel Anonymous." It read, "The glow of your halo is only exceeded by the size of your heart."

Let me share one of the many letters which she received. It is expressive of them all.

> One of the best directors this country has seen, and one of our best friends, has been Kathleen. Her sense of humor, her love and devotion, have managed to keep Southern middle in motion. For thirty-two years she has served our schools, "A balanced meal" her most important rule! When things went wrong, and the end looked near, Kathy was there to lend us an ear. The void she leaves, will be hard to fill, But, forget you, Kathleen? We never will! She taught Sunday School preschoolers for over thirty years. Katherine Russell, who had worked with her, said when her husband died, Kathleen Harris and Dr. Hubbard, the pastor then, were the first ones at their house. She said that Kathleen was a very dedicated and consecrated helper.

She and Ronald joined St. Matthews Baptist Church in 1950, members for 43 years. In the past, she sang in the choir, worked on the Food Services Committee, was President of the Ruth Sunday School Class, worked with GA's, active in WMU, was also a volunteer with her husband as a financial secretary of the church before the church had a paid worker. She served on many committees in the church.

Today we remember Kathleen as a loving wife, a marriage of fifty-four and a half years, a dedicated mother, grandmother, and as a kind and caring person. Many dubbed her "super woman" because she was able to do so many things. She was a hard worker who worked often from six to six. She was a perfectionist. She followed her mother's admonition, "Have everything perfect before you go to bed, because you never know what may happen." She loved her church, was active in it. She loved people, and they in turn loved her. We celebrate the wonderful gift of her life.

THE GIFT OF GOD'S SALVATION

Today we celebrate also the gift of God's salvation. Paul says, "Thanks be unto God for his unspeakable gift." Today we are assured that Kathleen has shared in this life eternal because of her deep faith in God. In a devotional she did for a class meeting she said: "Sometimes we see over a store the sign, 'Under New Management.' When we accept Christ as our Savior, our lives are under new management — God's management." And this was certainly true with her.

THE LORD TAKES AWAY — GRIEF.

The writer of Ecclesiastes reminds us that for everything there is a season, a time to be born, a time to die, a time to laugh, and a time to cry. Job knew that just as God gave the gift of life, so also suffering and death were a part of life. Today we acknowledge that life is filled with seasons that come and go. Winter has a certain beauty about it with its snow and coldness. But we delight in the returning to life in springtime. In spring buds break forth on the trees and new flowers arrive. We rejoice in the warmth and beauty of summer and in the dazzling colors of fall. As seasons come, change and go, they remind us of the mystery of life. Birth and death, laughter and sorrow are all a part of the mystery of life.

PAIN AND SUFFERING.

We know that God did not send the cancer upon Kathleen. Cancer is one of the mysteries of life, but it is a part of life just as health is. Kathleen inspired others by her faith and courage. When she got cancer, many thought she would only live a few months, but she lived five and a half years. Her deep faith, her will to live, her positive spirit and the prayers of others enabled her to go on. We also know that she inspired and helped many others. She received a certificate of appreciation, the Golden Rule Award, from *Friends for Life*, for the many persons she talked to who had cancer. Her inspiration helped them find courage. She told me a number of times that she was ready to go. Her faith was strong and whatever was the Lord's will she could accept. In her book of meditations, I found this selection which she evidently used a good bit. It reads:

What if we got exactly what we deserve in this life? What if we received only that which we have honestly earned? What a relief that this has not happened to us. We have received freely of the grace of God. We are blessed with the wonderful gift of what God has done for us. Unlike many material possessions, this gift is increased as it is shared. The more we seek to give to others, the more we have it in abundance.

Her faith enabled her to know that God always gives us far more than we deserve or have ever earned. We acknowledge that death is real and that our grief is real. It is O.K. to cry. Jesus stood by the grave of Lazarus and he too wept. We, too, know it is O.K. to weep. Crying is a normal part of our grief.

"BLESSED BE THE NAME OF THE LORD — GLORY."

Physical life is not the end. Kathleen loved to share and fix for others. Cooking meals was an important part of her life. She reminds me of Mary and Martha who often had Jesus into their home. Remember, that Jesus also came to their home when their brother Lazarus died. It was here that he said, "I am the resurrection and the life." We know that death is but a passageway from this life to the next. It is not a dead-end but an opportunity that goes further. Death opens a door from this physical world into the eternal world.

She trusted God and put her hand in his. She had a deep faith and she leaned back with quiet trust in God. When a person moves to another city, they usually transfer their letter to another church. Today Kathleen has transferred her letter from the church mortal to the church eternal, the physical church to the spiritual church — life everlasting. We recommend her with great joy!

HER LASTING INFLUENCE

Her influence for good will continue. The season of her influence will continue. Though she is no longer with us, the joy and happiness that she brought will be long remembered. She was a full-time mother and a full-time wife, as well as a full-time professional person. Her influence has been effective in so many areas. Just as the sun fades as it slowly sinks in the west and leaves an afterglow which we see for a long time after the sun has disappeared beyond the horizon, so Kathleen's influence for good, joy and radiance will continue to leave an afterglow among us. We shall feel her influence and presence into the tomorrows that lie ahead of us.

Jesus assured Mary at the grave of Lazarus that belief in him would lead to life everlasting. Today we trust with faith in that assurance. Death is a birthing from this life to the life beyond — the eternal life. I don't know what picture you have of life after death, but I don't think it is a picture of idleness. Kathleen, as much as she loved to be busy, would certainly not like to sit around and do nothing. I think she will find new opportunities to serve her Lord and grow in her devotion after death. And so calmly and quietly, today we note the home-going of this good woman-Kathleen Harris. May God give you the strength and comfort of his spirit to guide you as you face the future.

Eternal Father, bind up the broken hearts today with the balm of your presence. Draw Ronald, Audrey, the grandchildren, and other family members and friends close to yourself and may they sense your shepherding care and presence in the days ahead. May the memories of the good life with Kathleen and the assurance of life everlasting give to each of us in this hour comfort and assurance. Amen.

7.

A HOMILY

FOR

CONNIE BROWN
(THE DEATH OF A CHILD)

MARK 10:13-16

F ew experiences with death can be compared with the death of a child. When death snatches away one so young and innocent as Connie, our feelings of anguish and pain are overwhelming. We look into the empty bedroom and the vacant bed and know she will no longer be there. You had so many dreams for Connie's future but they will no longer be possible. Our heart aches with emotions and anger and our mind is filled with questions of why one so young should die. Even to raise such questions makes us feel guilty. But like the character Job in the Old Testament, who suffered in many ways, including the death of his children, we realize it is OK to raise such questions to God. In the midst of his tragedy, Job searched for answers to his suffering and grief, but no clear answers came to him. "I cry to you, O God," Job exclaimed, "and you do not answer me; I stand before you and you take no notice" (Job 30:20). Like Job it is OK to express your pain, anger, hurt and honest feelings at such a time as this. Although Job was a man of great faith, he dared to raise his questions to God. He was not ashamed of expressing his feelings to God and neither should you. Our emotions, created by God, are natural in the face of such a tragedy.

Questioning Is OK

Let me assure you today that it is alright to raise such questions to God. Neither you nor I will likely get the answers we want to the acute questions of undeserved suffering and death, nevertheless we cannot deny how we feel. Do not believe that it is a lack of faith to have such feelings and questions. They are not just your questions but mine and thousands of others. We long for simple answers to the mystery of evil and death, but those kinds of answers do not come. Some say, "Accept it. It is God's will." But I cannot believe that God deliberately wills the suffering and death of innocent children. God has created a world where suffering and death are realities, and I do not know why he created such a world. That's one of the questions I will raise with many others in the life beyond this one. God may not provide answers to all our questions, as he did not for Job, but he will come as the Answerer and Comforter as he did for Job.

A LESSON FROM DAVID

In 2 Samuel 12:15-23 an account is given of King David's grief at the death of his child by Bathsheba. When David learned that the child was ill, he prayed and fasted for the child's healing for seven days. After receiving word of the death of the child, rather than losing control of himself, David bathed, changed his clothes and went to the temple to worship God. He had prayed for the child to get well, but when that did not happen, he did not turn away from God but turned *to* God in worship for strength and comfort. He did not understand why his prayer was not answered as he voiced it for healing, yet he still trusted God even when his prayer was not granted as he desired. And so must we. No one has all the answers to the suffering and death of the innocent, yet we still must trust God. What other choice do we really have? Trust in God does not mean that we will always get what we pray for or always understand God's ways or will. Like David, I choose to lean in faith on God and not give way to despair or pessimism in the reality of suffering and death.

JESUS' LOVE FOR CHILDREN

The gospels record the disciples of Jesus attempting to keep children away from Jesus when he was teaching. Jesus told his disciples, "Let the children come to me, do not hinder them: for to such belongs the kingdom of God. Truly I say to you, whoever does not receive the kingdom of God like a child shall not enter it." And he took them in his arms and blessed them, laying his hands upon them. (Mark 10:14-16). In many children's departments in Sunday School, and even in some pediatric units in hospitals, you might see a painting of Jesus surrounded by small children and extending his arms to them. This is a pictorial message of Jesus' love for children. Without question Jesus had a special love for children, and we can be assured today that he feels your pain and grief at the death of Connie. Jesus, depicted as the Good Shepherd, reminds us of Isaiah's image "He will lead his flock like a shepherd, he will gather the lambs in his arms, he will carry them in his bosom." (Isaiah 40:11). Jesus has reached out his arms in love to embrace Connie and lead her into the house that God has prepared for all God's children. Such divine love should reassure us and comfort us in this time of grief. "Let the children come to me," Jesus said. The following hymn reminds us of Jesus' devotion to children.

> Jesus, Friend of little children,
> Be a friend to me;
> Take my hand and ever keep me.
> Close to Thee.
>
> Teach me how to grow in goodness,
> Daily as I grow;
> Thou hast been a child,
> And surely Thou dost know.
>
> Never leave me, nor forsake me,
> Ever be my Friend;
> For I need Thee, from life's dawning
> To the end.[4]

THE COMFORT OF GOD'S PRESENCE

Today we gather to reach for the comfort of God. We may not have all the answers to our questions about the suffering and death of innocent children, but we affirm that God is present with us and seeks to comfort us with that Presence. Isaiah has expressed that truth this way: "As one whom his mother comforts, so I will

---

4   Walter J. Mathams, "Jesus, Friend of Little Children," Cynthia Pearl Maus, *Christ and the Fine Arts* (New York: Harper & Brothers Publishers, 1938), 160.

comfort you." (Isaiah 66:13). Jesus assures us, "Blessed are those who mourn, for they shall be comforted." (Mathew 5:4). The Scriptures also remind us that "The eternal God is your dwelling place, and underneath are the everlasting arms." (Deuteronomy 33: 27). The 23rd Psalm reminds us that the Lord is our Shepherd and we shall not want. God is the One who comforts us with the assurance that not even death ultimately can separate us from those we love. God is the Comforter and the One that helps us bear the pain of our grief. We may not have all the answers to our many questions, but we have the *Presence* of *the Answerer* to comfort us. I pray that the assurance of that divine love will sustain and comfort you now. George Matheson reminds us of the extent of that love:

> O love that will not let me go,
> I rest my weary soul in thee;
> I give thee back the life I owe,
> That in thine ocean depths its flow
> May richer fuller be.
>
> O Joy that seekest me through pain
> I cannot close my heart to thee;
> I trace the rainbow through the rain,
> And feel the promise is not vain
> That morn shall tearless be.[5]

> *O loving Father, who loves us as his own children, bind up our broken hearts in the balm of your healing love. Give us strength and grace to follow you in the days ahead, until we pass into that heavenly home you have prepared for all us and are reunited with Connie and all those we love. Amen.*

---

5   George Matheson, "O Love that Wilt Not Let Me Go," *Ibid.*, 232.

8.

A Homily

for

Alfred Leland
(A Faithful Minister)

2 Timothy 4:6-8

This afternoon we are gathered here to pay tribute to a departed loved one, Dr. Alfred Leland, Sr. We have gathered to express our grief and to sense the presence of God. We acknowledge our sadness but celebrate the gift of his life. We acknowledge that our grief and pain are real, but we also affirm our faith and hope today. The Apostle Paul said, "I have fought the good fight, I have finished the course, I have kept the faith. Henceforth there is laid up for me a crown of righteousness, which the Lord the righteous judge will award me on that day, not only to me but also to all who love his appearing" (2 Timothy 4:6-8).

These words to Timothy were among Paul's last words to his friends. The last words from anyone mean a great deal as we reflect on that individual's life. Today we gather in this service of worship in gratitude for the life of Al Leland and in celebration of the resurrection faith. Let us follow Paul's words to guide us.

"I Have Fought the Good Fight."

Since Al served in such a quiet way within our church after he retired, many people were unaware of his education. He prepared himself well. He was a graduate of Georgetown College, received the Bachelor of Theology and Master of Theology degrees from Southern Seminary. He studied under such noted professors as John Sampey, Kyle Yates and J. McKee Adams. He wrote a Master's thesis entitled, *Men of the Spirit: A Study of Job and the Prophets.* Later he earned a Doctor of Theology degree. He was a learned man and learned five different languages in college and seminary. Although he was well learned, he was a humble man and did not wear his education on his sleeves. He said titles were not important. To him, it was not important that people knew about his background.

He served as pastor of the First Baptist Church in Greensburg, Indiana for several years. He was an Army Air Force Chaplain during World War II for five years. He served in some dangerous situations and was almost killed several times. He told me on numerous occasions that it was only the grace of God that brought him through some of these conflicts and he knew that God had saved him for some future service. I saw a Certificate of Appreciation for his military service which hung on his wall.

He served for many years as sales manager for Belknap Hardware. He was a charter founder of Lyndon Volunteer Fire Department and served them for almost fifty years, at times as secretary and treasurer. One of his daughters told me how she remembered how handsome he looked in that volunteer fire department uniform when she was a small child. We pay high respect today for one who served his Lord faithfully. He was a man who lived what he believed. His life reflected what he said. He was a committed Christian who served God whether it was in the front of people or in a quiet way. He fought the fight of faith with courage and conviction.

"I Have Finished the Course."

Al did not just begin. He was one who continued what he started. His whole life was a continuation of service and ministry to his family, friends, church and business. He endured to the end. He finished the course. When St. Matthews Baptist Church burned, he like many others wept because of the loss. But he stood by his church and prayed for it and continued to attend and gave financial support. He was one of our strong saints who held up the church during a difficult time.

Many things helped Al finish the course. Let me list some of these.

1) He knew who he was. He was seen by friends and family as honest, articulate, and forthright. People knew where he stood. He did not hesitate to let you know what he thought and what he believed.

2) He was a humble man. He never pushed himself or his education, but in his own quiet way he served God.

3) He had a deep faith in God. In one of his sermons based on Acts 7:54-60 entitled, "Looking Up" he speaks about Stephen's

faith. He said, "Stephen had an unfaltering trust in Christ." He addressed his Master as Lord Jesus. This brought him a great sense of calm and there was with this a certain hope of faith so that he was able to commend his spirit to the Father. He says that "this is a proper model for the dying Christian" and it has been a proper model for Al throughout his life and also in his dying.

4) Love helped carry him through. His love was exhibited for his family and others.

He was a loving husband; a caring loving father, grandfather, and great-grandfather. He was always there in times of need for his family. He was a wonderful counselor and a wonderful listener and the children would come to him. He would give good advice, wise, and helpful. He was one who put his family first.

Al was a person who wanted to give his life in helping others and he did this through love. He believed in loving his neighbor, his fellow man and woman as well as his family. He put into practice the great passage from 1 Corinthians 13. He knew that love was that quality which made one like God because he knew that God is love, and he that loves not, does not know God. He believed that love begets love and that we love because God first loved us. Love gave joy in his heart, enabled him to be energetic and reach out with courteous, gracious ways toward others.

Another one of his sermons was entitled, "The Vastness of Love," based on Psalm 90 and 1 Corinthians 2:9-10. He points out that God loves those who love him and that God's love is not in word only. He reminds us that God loved so much that he gave, and that real genuine love is known in our living. "By their fruits you shall know them." He spoke of the great joy of sharing this love with others.

5) He was a creative person. His family said that they thought he could do anything. He was so skilled and handy in so many ways. He had been a draftsman — designed the blueprints for his own house. He was a craftsman — able to make almost anything. His woodworking skills were seen in the beautiful doll houses, model ships and other things that he made. Anytime he was asked

to help, he was always there. When his children were small, they spoke about school projects he helped them with like designing a stagecoach from Valentines which helped them win first place. Or a leaf collection where each leaf was placed on a hand cutout page shaped like a leaf by him. He was always willing to share his handyman gifts with others.

6) He was an encourager. He was an encourager to others and to me. In many ways he was a Barnabas, a son of encouragement. Every time he spoke to me he said some words to try to lift my spirit and to let me know of his supportive spirit. He did that not only for me but for many others.

"I Have Kept the Faith."

Al was a man of deep faith. It was a quiet faith, but it was real in his life. We gather today acknowledging that life will be different without this good man among us and we are grieved by his loss. He will leave a vacuum but we know that his faith was real and strong and that he would want us to have a faith that is real and strong.

He faced suffering and cancer with courage. I do not know why cancer and pain are a part of life. I do know that God does not send this deliberately upon us. I believe that without the possibility of suffering and pain, there could be no growth or maturing. Like a small child, we place our hand in God and lean upon him in trust and strength and I know that Al believed this as well.

In his Th.M. thesis on Job, in a section entitled "A New View of Suffering" in the Book of Job, he wrote: "Afflictions may be sent upon the righteous as a trial of their faith. If patiently borne, they lead to a higher knowledge of God, a deepening of trust, a beautifying of character and other rewards. They do not mean that God is angry with his servants. Moreover, God wishes his servants to trust him, even in the dark. He does not try to vindicate his ways by argument, but shows himself to the sufferer, that he may widen and deepen his thought of God's greatness. We can well afford to leave our case with the wise Creator and preserver of all things.

Trust him always and everywhere!" This is an indication of his assurance and trust in God.

WE KNOW THAT IT IS OK TO CRY.

Jesus wept by the grave of his friend Lazarus and it is OK for us to share our grief. We grieve not as those who have no hope, but those who trust in God. In sermon notes of Al, I found these words that he wrote about tears: "In moments when tears cloud the eyes and sorrows cover the heart — it is hard to see the miracle of God's love. But yet we can still have that 'peace be still' within us. Jesus reminded us 'you believe in God believe in me.' How often the Master sought the quietness of the garden and under the old olive trees he poured out his heart and said 'not my will but thine.' Jesus reminds us that this is the Father's will and that he has gone to prepare a place for us." In quietness and trust he leaned upon his Lord.

Al believed in service. He had served God in his church where he was pastor, as a chaplain, through his business, and through his own way as a volunteer in our church here at St. Matthews. He had served in many ways on our Deacon Nominating Committee, as President of the Areopagus Sunday School Class, as an usher, and in many other ways. One of the last things he said to me in the hospital was; "Pastor, when I get well, I want to help you visit in the hospital."

I remember after I had only been here a short while that Al stopped by one day and gave me his small communion set that he had used while he was in the service. He thought that I might be able to use it. I still remember his sense of graciousness to me. As I use that communion set today to serve others, I remember how many he has served with it in the past and it will be a means of his continuing to serve today.

"THERE IS LAID UP FOR HIM A CROWN OF RIGHTEOUSNESS."

Today we affirm our faith and hope in life after death. We believe that Jesus has gone to prepare a place for us. We acknowledge today the birthing of the life of Al to the life eternal. Death is not the end but the beginning of a new life. This good man, who lived his life in faith and died in faith, has now gone to live eternally with the God he loved. Al LeLand has transferred his letter from the church mortal to the church immortal, from flesh to the spiritual life.

We are approaching Easter Sunday, that wondrous event in the life of the church. Al had a sermon, "I Am the Resurrection," based on 1 Corinthians 15 and John 11. He said "because Jesus Christ lives we know that we shall live also. We find in him the reality of life. We seek a living union with Christ. We know that our redeemer lives, peace is God's gift to us out of his love and that Jesus has not left us comfortless, that he has gone to prepare a place for us and we know because of his resurrection that we have assurance of life everlasting."

In some sermon notes on the sunset and evening star, Al says that "death is not an entrance into an unfathomable void but a promise of a new sunrise tomorrow. The sunrise that shall find us in the city that is four square. He says that when we go there, we shall be able to echo the words of Jesus in Luke 23:28 "Daughters of Jerusalem weep not for me but weep for yourselves and for your children." To the Christian, this is the moment for which we have waited, the day for which we planned the end of which we have dreamed. Sunset and evening star, sunset is not the end but is the promise of a new sunrise tomorrow." It is a birthing from this life to life eternal.

There is no question that Al lived his life by faith. He also believed that when he lay down to die he too would go forth to meet his master with the assurance of the gracious love and presence of Christ. Now that Al Leland has departed from this life, he will leave an impact that will continue to be seen. His goodness, love, encouragement, hope and faith will shine in our lives and in the lives of others. We are better persons because we have known him.

At the conclusion of his Th.M. thesis, Al quoted a hymn from Isaac Watts. I think these lines are expressive also about his faith. Listen to these words:

> I'm not ashamed to own my Lord,
> Or to defend His cause,
> Maintain the honor of His Word,
> The glory of His cross.
> Jesus, my God,
> I know His name;
> His name is all my trust;
> Nor will He put my soul to shame.
> Nor let my soul be lost.
> Firm as His throne His promise stands.
> And He can well secure
> What I've committed to His hands
> Till the decisive hour.
> Then will He own my worthless name
> Before His Father's face,
> And in the New Jerusalem
> Appoint my soul a place. Amen.[6]

Loving God, bind up the broken hearts today with the balm of Your presence. Draw Lucy, Suzan, Debra, Al, Jr., Steve, the grandchildren, great-grandchildren and other members of the family close to Yourself and may they sense Your shepherding care and presence in the days ahead. May the memories of the good life with Al and the assurance of life everlasting give to each of us in this hour comfort and assurance. Amen.

---

6   Isaac Watts, "I'm Not Ashamed to Own My Lord," *Trinity Hymnal*, Revised Edition (Suwanee, GA: Great Commission Publishers, 1990), 505.

9.

A HOMILY
FOR
HENRY FEATHERS
(A COMMUNITY SERVANT)

"IN GOD'S HANDS"

"We know that to them that love God all things work together
for good to them who are called according to his purpose."
Romans 8:28

This was Henry's favorite verse.

ALL THINGS

Henry discovered early that life was not always easy or painless. He knew joy and pleasure but he also experienced difficulty and illness. Before he was twelve years old he fell out of the tobacco barn and didn't tell his mother. He broke a rib and punctured a lung. Later when his school tested him for TB, they thought he contracted it because of a lung scar and spot. He spent one and a half years in a TB hospital. At a young age, he experienced loneliness and separation from family as well as fear and pain. God didn't send this upon him, but he learned from this accident and became a stronger person spiritually. He often experienced poor health, but he did not become pessimistic. He had a great sense of humor and loved to tell jokes.

Paul reminds us that all things strengthen a person's life- not just trials, losses and suffering. Health, happiness, love, a good job, strong family and friends, good parents, a good mind and dedicated spirit add to our growth. Henry's dedicated service of over 32 years with the US Public Health Service and a consultant for 4 or 5 years later enriched his life as he helped others.

All things-

His life was fortified by 49 years of marriage to Connie, with their 2 children-Debra and James and one child deceased, 6 grandchildren and 6 great grandchildren. He was also dedicated to community service and was a past president of the Lions Club. He received the Jack Stickly Fellowship Award for dedicated humanitarian service. He always put his family first. He used to say: "Children didn't ask to be put on earth, so we have to care for them." He was a loving husband, father and friend to many.

Work Together for Good

This does not mean that all things that happen are good or that God sends all things upon us, but that all things, "work together" for the ultimate good. Paul is reminding us to take a "long view." We have to remember that God has a goal to make us better persons not merely comfortable and happy persons. Our world is a place to train us morally and spiritually. It is a school for character and faith development where we grow after God's purpose not our own. We strive to be like Christ.

All things are for good because they help us learn from our suffering, pain and mistakes, instead of complaining about them. Henry overcame many illnesses and had eight or nine surgeries. Henry taught his children and used to remind them frequently, "We live in God's hands. Do not pray to have your burdens removed but to be in God's hands. Seek God's guidance and strength." By his life and words, he lived and taught this lesson to his family.

Those That Love God

Paul had spoken before about God's love for us, but here in this Roman letter is the only place that he spoke of our love to God. In many ways, Henry showed his love for God. He showed his love through his dedicated vocation for thirty-two years as a Public Health Official. He cared for others and taught them to live better lives. He showed his love for God through his love for his family. When Hank was ordained he said that the most important people in his life were his parents. What a strong witness this is! Henry's love had a great impact upon him. We saw his love for God through his dedicated community service. He served through the Lions Club, the Shriners and Masons and in other ways. We saw his love for God through his dedicated church ministry as a Deacon and in his faithful attendance in worship and Sunday School. Henry was there faithfully, even on Wednesday nights. He showed his love for God by his high moral ideals and strong character. His life showed what he believed. He lived what he taught. Although

Henry was a quiet reserved man who never raised his voice, he was indeed a man of few words, but he was a gentleman-a gentle man. He had quiet strength within his inner being.

During these many months of his illness, no one could have asked anyone to have been more loving than his family was for him. Connie, Debra, Hank and the grandchildren faithfully supported, encouraged and tended to him during this time.

We Know

This is Paul's ringing cry of certainty. Paul often used this phrase. "We know the whole of creation groans in travail as it moves toward fulfillment." "We know the earthly house of this tabernacle is dissolved and we have a building from God." "I know whom I have believed . . ." Paul affirmed that nothing could separate us from God when we were in Jesus Christ. His love sustained us. Paul lived and died with that kind of certainty and so did Henry.

In one of the stories about Alfred Lord Tennyson, there is an episode where he is walking one day in a beautiful flower garden with a friend. His friend said to him, "Mr. Tennyson, you speak often of Jesus; can you tell me what Christ means to your life?" Tennyson had been walking and he stopped and pointed to a beautiful yellow flower, "What the sun is to that flower," Tennyson said, "Christ is to my soul." A person could see beauty in that flower because it had responded to the light and warmth of the sun above. So our life as it responds to the Son of God and the light from him shows the beauty of God and we have confidence because we walk with God.

Henry trusted God and leaned in quiet faith and inner assurance. As Christians we affirm that death is not the end. It is not a dead end street but a doorway to new life. Henry's suffering and pain are over. He is now with the God he loves. The flowers today represent the love of the family, but they also symbolize the resurrection garden. This is the garden where Jesus said, "Because

I live, you will also." Jesus said, "I have gone to prepare a place for you," and so we know that Jesus has gone to prepare that place for Henry and he now dwells eternally in God's love.

We close the service with a prayer that Henry wrote himself. The prayer reads as follows:

> O God and Father of us all,
> Upon thy boundless mercy do we call,
> Be with us as we leave this meeting
> And continue the activities of the evening.
>
> Give us courage to perform our duties,
> Let us maintain confidence in each other.
> Keep our bodies well and strong and
> Make our minds sound and clear.
>
> Help us to keep our hearts clean, and
> Strive to live honestly and fearlessly
> Open our eyes that we may see good in all things.
> Grant us new visions of thy truth and joy
>
> In the name of our Lord and Savior
> Jesus Christ, Amen.

A Homily

for

Jane Pageant
(A Long Illness)

"The One Sacrament of Life"

John 14:1-6, 25-27

T his afternoon we have gathered to remember and celebrate the gift of the life of Jane Pageant.

IMPACT OF LOVE

Jane was a person who knew and practiced the importance of love in her life. She loved her family and was a devoted wife to her husband, John, who died in 1973, and was a dedicated mother to Jane and John her children and to her grandchildren. They lovingly cared for her during her illness, especially Jane. She loved her friends and communicated to her family, especially her grandchildren, the importance of friends. Jane loved people and enjoyed being with them and meeting new people. She never met a stranger. She always reached out with a warm handshake and a friendly smile.

She loved life. On her mirror she had posted these two notes which indicate her philosophy of life. "Love is a fabric which never fades, no matter how often it is washed in the water of adversity and grief." "A man (or woman) of words and not of deeds is like a garden full of weeds." *English Proverb*.

Jane loved music. She enjoyed playing the piano and still played her recital pieces until recently. She instilled in her children and grandchildren a love for music. She loved sports- swimming, diving, tennis, golf, dancing and playing cards. She enjoyed puzzles, scrabble and crossword puzzles. Jane loved to read books and talk about them. She also loved to travel and learn about places and people. Family and friends remember her wonderful sense of humor and know she could tell a good story and share a good joke. She loved life and lived it full and well.

The following is a poem she had in her Bible from *Charity and Children*, Nov. 28, 1982-

Take time to work- it is the price of success
Take time to think- it is the source of power
Take time to play- it is the secret of youth
Take time to read- it is the fountain of knowledge
Take time to worship- it washes the dust of earth from our eyes
Take time to help and enjoy friends- it is the source of happiness
Take time to love- it is the one sacrament of life
Take time to dream- it hitches the soul to the stars
Take time to laugh- it is the singing that helps with life's loads
Take time to plan- it is the secret of being able
to have time to take time for the first nine points.

JANE LOVED TEACHING.

She taught math and chemistry for 27 years. Students who sat in her geometry class said she had high expectations, but she made it fun and the subject came alive under her teaching. Her classes were never dull, but vibrant and helpful. One of her former students who is now in public education sent her this note when she was ill recently. It is a powerful word of affirmation about her and her teaching gifts.

You have touched the lives of so many individuals (students) in such a positive way. Whenever I think of my teachers you are the first to come to my mind. You had such high standards for all your students and I thank you for caring. I thank you for not accepting mediocrity. I thank you for believing in me when I didn't believe in myself. You have been an outstanding role model. I like to think that my successes have been in no small part a result of the effect you had on my life. I sincerely wish you well! May God richly bless you as you have been a blessing to me.

After hearing a sermon I preached one Sunday about many of us waiting too late to express appreciation to those who have had a positive impact on us, one of our members as he left the church pulled Jane aside and said, "I want to thank you for the wonderful influence you had on me. I wanted to tell you before it's too late." She laughed, smiled and thanked him.

SHE LOVED HER CHURCH AND CHURCH FAMILY.

She was active in Baptist Women and taught in the Children's Department in Sunday School for over 20 years. Her Bible is filled with notes in the margin where she read and studied it carefully. She was faithful in her church attendance and strong support of her church.

The words from the fourteenth chapter of John give us some sources to help us as we face our grief. First, Jesus said, "Let not your heart be troubled." Our faith in Christ dispels our fear. We lean back in quiet trust on God. Jesus assured his disciples, and us, that even when our heart is troubled God is with us. Our hearts are sad, but they are not broken. We are thankful that Jane's suffering is over and she is gone to be with the God she loved. We remember the loving care she received from Jane, John, Kitty and her grandchildren. We know that life will be different now without her. We will miss her, but we would not want her to be back to suffer. Our hearts are at peace because we know that God is with us. In one of her notes in her Bible she had written the following lines:

> "None of us lives to himself and
> none of us dies to himself
> We are bound together in the bundle of life.
>
> If we live, we live to the Lord,
> If we die, we die to the Lord
> So then whether we live or die
> We are the Lord's.

BELIEVE IN GOD

Second, Jesus said, "Believe in God." We lean back in faith on God to know that we face our grief not alone, but God's everlasting arms are underneath us and God is there to sustain us. Jane loved music and especially Zollene Reissner's organ playing (the organist at our church), the music programs, anthems, and solos at church. When she was too ill to go to church, she would listen at home and she would sing along with the hymns and pray the Lord's prayer with us.

BELIEVE IN ME

Third, Jesus said, "Believe also in me." Jesus had revealed to us what God is like. God is love, grace, concern, and care. Jesus is the good shepherd and cares for us, and walks with us through this grief. Just as a child lifts up its hand to put it in its father's or mother's hand for guidance through an unknown place, so today, quietly, Jane has placed her hand in the hand of Christ, to walk into that place that He has prepared.

When I first visited Jane in the hospital and she had the first hint that her problem might be serious, she said to me, "I have lived 84 good, wonderful years. Whatever the outcome is I am ready." That's a strong faith!

MANY ROOMS

Fourth Jesus said, "In my father's house are many rooms." Today Jane has a home going. She has gone to that place that Christ has prepared. Her suffering is over. She has gone to rest where there is joy and peace. Jesus has assured us, "If this were not so, I would have told you." The flowers today symbolize not only the love of family and friends, but the resurrection garden. We know death is not the end. There is a homing instinct in all of us that draws us to God. We know that God knows Jane and she is there in the home that God has prepared. There is room for all.

MY PEACE

Fifth, Jesus said, "My peace I leave with you." The peace of Jesus gives us inner strength and his peace sustains us. We reach out now in our grief to draw upon the power of His presence. We know that our strength is not enough, but we reach out to Him.

A PREPARED PLACE

Sixth, Jesus said, "I have gone to prepare a place for you." This is a definite place where we will rest from our labors, difficulties, and pain. We know that Jane is now home in this heavenly place that our Lord has provided. Death is not a wall, but a door. Death is not a dead-end, but a new pathway to God. Death is not an end, but a beginning. Jesus said, "Because I live, you shall live also." We know today that Jane has gone to be with the God she loves. Death is a birthing from this life to the next one.

In her Bible Jane had written this prayer. It is an affirmation of her faith and assurance in God's eternal love and grace. "O Lord, support us all the day long, until the shadows lengthen and the evening comes, and the busy world is hushed, and the fever of life is over, and our work is done. Then in thy mercy grant us a safe lodging, and a holy rest, and peace at the last. Amen."

Jane loved Zollene's organ music and especially her benediction. The family asked her to play it this afternoon. Zollene wrote the words and the music. Listen to the words and then celebrate the music and the testimony it proclaims.

> As a light comes through the darkness,
> As the rain falls on a dry and dusty day,
> As the fire's warmth comes to one who knows the cold,
> So may God's love come to you.
>
> As the green blade pushes through the crusted earth,
> As the flower opens from the tight-wrapped bud,
> As kindness comes to one who has been lonely,
> So may God's love come.
>
> As a breeze comes through the stillness,
> As comfort comes to one who knows life's pain,
> As love comes anew to a heart grown cold,

So may God's love come,
So may Christ's love come,

May the peace of God's love come to you today.
Alleluia, Alleluia, Amen.

11.

A HOMILY

FOR

MICHAEL ALLEN TUCK
(MOTORCYCLE ACCIDENT)

PSALM 45 AND PSALM 130

W e come to this moment with out hearts filled with shock, grief and denial. That such an accident can happen so quickly and without warning leaves us groping for an-swers. We know that no words can adequately express our deep feelings of despondency and heartache today. To have one we love to be snatched away by this terrible accident leaves us overwhelmed with emotions of all kinds, grief, anger, frustration, and others unexpressed. We can't understand it all. Suffering and death have no easy word. There is no right word for such a time as this. We acknowledge our deep loss and our search for comfort at such a time as this. Where do we turn for comfort?

We Stand before the Mystery of Death

We gather today first of all acknowledging the mystery of life. For all of us there is a sense of shock and denial, some sense of de-pression, physical symptoms, and even some hostility. Questions run through our minds. Why is there suffering and pain? Why does God allow such accidents to happen? These are your questions and my questions. We acknowledge that we cannot understand all of the mystery of life. But we have to acknowledge that death is not the only mystery of life. Birth itself is a mystery. So is the beauty of fall, the coldness of winter, the budding of life in the spring, and the warmth of summer. There is mystery in birth and growing, in lov-ing and caring. The buds on the trees in the springtime of the year remind us that life goes on. They have been dormant all through winter, but the warmth of spring brings them back to life. Flowers blossom forth from the seeds and bulbs that have been planted so that we have their loveliness in the summer. No one can explain so easily how life continues or why it ends as it does. There is a deep sense of mystery in so much of life beyond suffering and death.

THANKFUL FOR THE GIFT OF LIFE

Secondly, we thank God for the gift of life. We thank God for the years we shared with Mike. We remember the joys and happiness as well as the difficult days. Those who knew Mike well recognized his sense of independence. He loved life and enjoyed it to its fullest. Motorcycles were a great love of his life, and he was talented in fixing them as few people are. He was a mechanical genius. One time, following a wreck on a race track, someone suggested that they just pick up the pieces and throw the bike away. But Mike gathered up the pieces and put it together again.

He seemed to know the right thing to do. He was the type who, when he set out on a project, saw it through. He did not give up. He was not a quitter. Although he liked to be a clown at times, in his quiet way he was a leader. He was a person of few words, but he had a clever way of saying things. He was thoughtful of others especially in little things. If you needed help, he was always willing to give a hand. He was there when needed. He did not receive compliments well and did not like to be fussed over. He expressed his own affection in quiet unpretentious ways. During these days of grief, friends have said to the family: "Your son made our life brighter. He always had something cute to say."

We shall remember his big appetite and unlike some of us, he never gained weight. We remember how he loved to put up the Christmas tree. Christmas was a special time for him. Friends and customers in the motorcycle shop respected his judgment and trusted him personally. They knew he was a good man. He often said to neighbors or friends who had a problem with a bike, "Can I help you?" It was his nature to want to help. We will miss him. Life will not be the same. But the good memory of his life will remain in our heart and memory. His good will lives on.

THE GOODNESS OF GOD

Third, we continue to affirm the goodness of God, even in the face of death. We reaffirm our faith today in the goodness of

God and rest on the conviction that his love is eternal and strong. God created life out of his love and God sustains it. We do not know why God has created the possibility of accidents like this happening. They are a part of the universe God has created. Without the possibility of suffering and pain, there could be no growth or maturing. We know that God does not deliberately send these things upon us. Today like a small child we place our hand in the hand of God to lean upon him for trust and strength. We know our strength is not enough. We have no easy answers but acknowledge our need for the support and grace of God in such a time as this.

The Dark Valley of Grief

Fourth. We know that family and friends are walking through a dark valley of grief. But we come to this valley of grief armed with the assurance that God is present with us. A favorite writer of mine, Harry Emerson Fosdick, who went through a deeply personal tragic experience, wrote once: "It was the most terrifying wilderness I ever traveled through. I dreadfully wanted to commit suicide. But instead I made one of the most vital discoveries in my life. I found God in a desert." Sometimes our deepest insights are discovered in the darkest valley. We find that in the midst of despair, pain, and suffering that God is there. Even when we do not know it or feel it, God is there. We grieve but we grieve not as those who have no hope. We grieve with a sense of trust in the presence of God who is with us even when we are too numb to sense it.

Weeping with Hope

Fifth, we weep today, but we weep not as those who have no hope. We acknowledge that it is all right to cry. It is O. K. to acknowledge that we have sorrow at Mike's passing, but we do not grieve as those who have no hope. Death and the grave are not the end for the Christian. Jesus himself wept beside the grave of his friend Lazarus, and so we know it is good to express our grief and not to keep it deep down inside of us. We acknowledge that we grieve because life will be different without Mike. Twenty-three years were shared with him, and we shall miss him. But we shall be able to face life and go on, because we have the presence of God and the support of family and friends with us. We acknowledge that although he is no longer with us, he is present with God where there is no suffering or pain.

THE ASSURANCE OF A NEW BEGINNING

Sixth, we come also to thank God today for the assurance of peace which we have from Christ. Today we rest on the promise of life eternal through Christ. Our great sorrow is to be separated from Mike, but we have the assurance today that through faith in Jesus Christ he dwells in that marvelous eternal realm with him. As we lean upon God in faith, we know that one day we shall join him in the eternal realm where there is no hurt or sorrow but only peace. We thank God that death is not the end but a new beginning. The flowers present today are a sign of the love and devotion of friends and family. But they also symbolize for us the resurrection garden on Easter Day when Jesus Christ himself rose from the grave. They give to us an assurance that death is not the end but a doorway that opens from this life to a new life where the spiritual person is with God. Jesus said, "I have gone to prepare a place for you." He has gone to prepare that place for Mike, and Mike is there with God where he will dwell eternally in the home which he has made. We, of course, shall miss him, but today we rest with the assurance that he is with Christ and dwells eternally with him without pain and suffering. Each of us one day shall join him. Jesus said, "Because I live you shall live also."

Pearl Buck once wrote a remarkable story a number of years ago entitled *The Big Wave*. In this story a young mother has died and the father is talking with his small children. One of them asked: "Daddy, what is it like to die?" The father responds by saying to his child: "Son, do you remember when you were born?" "No, Daddy, I don't remember that. I was too small." "Well, son," the father continues, "when you came into the world, you left a world in your mother's body where your every need was met. You were perfectly content. For you to leave that world and come into this world was a great shock. It was a kind of death. You did not know that on this side you had a loving mother and father waiting for you who were going to care for you and love you." Death is like that. It is a birthing from this life to the spiritual life. There we meet God. Our loving Father, who awaits us - to give us a new and abundant life, that is beyond our imagination. Death is a birthing from this life to the eternal life. Today we affirm our hope and assurance in life everlasting. For us as Christians, death is a birth from this world to the next. May God give us the sense to know that his presence and assurance are with us today and in the weeks ahead.

One of my favorite poets is John Donne. Let me share these words from him with you.

> "Death, be not proud, though some have called thee
> Mighty and dreadful, for thou art not so;
> For those whom thou think'st thou dost overthrow
> Die not, poor Death; nor yet canst thou kill me.
> From Rest and Sleep, which but thy picture be,
> Much pleasure, then from thee much more must flow;
> And soonest our best men with thee do go —
> Rest of their bones and souls' delivery!
> Thou'rt slave to fate, chance, kings, and desperate men,
> And dost with poison, war and sickness dwell;
> And poppy or charms can make us sleep as well
> And better than thy stroke. Why swell'st thou then?
> One short sleep past, we wake eternally;
> And Death shall be no more; Death, thou shalt die![7]

Eternal Redeemer, bind up the broken hearts today with the balm of your presence. Draw Preston, Betty, Vicki, Steve and other family members and friends close to yourself and may they sense your shepherding care and presence in the days ahead. May the memories of the good life with Mike

---

7   John Donne, "Death," Morrison, *Masterpieces of Religious Verse*, 617.

and the assurance of life everlasting give to each of us in this hour comfort and assurance. Through Christ we pray. Amen.

12.

A HOMILY
FOR
ALICE CONRAD
(SIX YEARS OF ILLNESS)

EPHESIANS 5:20

The apostle Paul writes to one of the young churches and says "In all things give thanks." It is easy for us to give thanks on warm beautiful days but when it is a cold, damp, rainy day like today, it is much more difficult. It is easy for us to give thanks when things are going well in life and we are joyful and happy. But when our lives are filled with pain, grief and suffering it is more difficult. Paul has admonished us to learn to give thanks in all things. Let's see if we can pause today and think of some things for which we are thankful as we face our grief.

THE GIFT OF LIFE

First of all, thank God for the gift of life. All life comes to us as a gift. Today we pause to remember the years that were shared with Alice. We remember the joys and sorrows, the hopes and difficulties, the blessings and struggles. We know that she loved life and rejoiced in it. She was a homemaker. Her home was very important to her. She always kept a neat, lovely home. She loved to cook, especially at Christmastime. She would have special parties and cook foods that family members would love. The family remembers especially, her wonderful chocolate pie. Alice lived in the country, but she was a person who loved the town. She was a social person who liked being around other people. She had a good time with her family. She and her sisters were close and they loved to be together, and they would cut up and laugh and talk. They all loved to go to the beach, where they could spend time together. White Lake was also another favorite spot for family and friends. Family members could always have a good time with her. We thank God for the wonderful gift of her life and the years that family and friends could share with her.

Alice was a positive, outgoing and lively person. She loved to give gifts to family and friends at birthdays and Christmas. She also liked to be the person who picked up the bill when they went out to eat. She was a giving, free hearted person. Alice was also demonstrative in her affection. She would tell you that she loved you. David was "the light of her life." She was thrilled to have a son and much of her life centered around him. She would brag about him and talk about him with family and friends. She also loved her five grandchildren. She said that Carol was her favorite granddaughter. Of course, Carol was her only granddaughter, but she was still her favorite.

Punctual was a word, the family said, was always true about Alice. She was always on time, in fact sometimes she would be a half hour early when you invited her to come to your home. She didn't put off anything, she was always working ahead. Alice enjoyed her Sunday School class when she was able to go. She read her Bible faithfully and used to love to sing and listen to Julie play the piano. She liked music very much. It was a vital part of her life.

Weeping Is OK

Second, we thank God that we can weep today, but not as those without hope. We know that Jesus wept beside the grave of his good friend Lazarus. So it is okay for us to express our grief. God does not want us to bury it deep down inside of us, because we know that life will be different without Alice. Alice had been ill for about six years. Her family had cared for her lovingly. David had given devoted love and attention to her. We know that her suffering and pain are over and she has gone to be with God. We can be thankful that she has now passed this stage and is free of all of her suffering.

God's Presence

Third, we thank God today for the assurance of God's presence during our time of suffering and grief. We know that we do not have to bear our grief and pain alone, that Christ, the Good Shepherd, is here with us. We can lean upon him because we know that we draw strength from his presence to help us through our struggles. We lean upon each other knowing that family and friends will help us bear the load. We cast our burden upon the

Lord because we know that he will sustain us and give us strength and comfort.

A poem that tells us about God supporting us during difficult times is "Footprints"

> One night a man had a dream. He dreamed he
> Was walking along the beach with the Lord.
> Across the sky flashed scenes from his life.
> For each scene, he noticed two sets of footprints
> In the sand: one belonging to him, and the other
> To the Lord.
>
> When the last scene of his life flashed before
> Him, he looked back at the footprints in the
> Sand. He noticed that many times along the path
> Of his life there was only one set of footprints.
> He also noticed that it happened at the very lowest
> And saddest times in his life.
>
> This really bothered him and he questioned the
> Lord about it. "Lord, you said that once
> I decided to follow you, you'd walk with me all the
> Way. But I have noticed that during the most
> Troublesome times in my life, there is only one set
> Of footprints. I don't understand why when I needed
> You most you would leave me."
>
> The Lord replied, "My son, My precious child,
> I love you and I would never leave you. During your
> Times of trial and suffering, when you see only one
> Set of footprints, it was then that I carried you.[8]

---

8 Mary Stevenson, "Footprints in the Sand," *Footprints in the Sand Website.*

We are assured that when life is more difficult than we can bear, the Lord has undergirded us and is bearing us up during our difficulties and tragedies. We can be thankful for that assurance.

DEATH IS A DOORWAY

Fourth, we thank God that death is not a wall, but it is a door, a doorway that leads from this life to the eternal life. Death is not a dead end, but a new beginning. The flowers that are given by family and friends symbolize not only love, but they remind us of the resurrection garden. Jesus said, "I have gone to prepare a place for you." "Because I live, you shall live also." Quietly and peacefully today, we lean back today in the assurance that Alice has gone to that eternal home that God has prepared for her and for all those who love him.

Robert Louis Stevenson relates in one of his stories about a lad who was shipwrecked on a small island off the coast of Scotland. Across an angry sea, he could see a farmhouse where help could be found. Isolated by this fuming sea, despair and fear set in. But he discovered at low tide that the sea that separated him from life and hope was shallow enough to be waded across. "The terror he felt was only make-believe, Stevenson said. Isn't that the Christian word of victory in the face of death—the terror is only make-believe. Jesus Christ gives us the victory that overcomes our fears and pain. We live in a world that is familiar, and we feel secure in it. But then one day, when death comes, we are suddenly thrust from this familiar material world into a new world where the "sea" seems to wide to cross. We need to remember that on the other side of this "sea" there is a loving God, our family and friends who are waiting for us and a life filled with tenderness, love and grace.

So today, quietly and serenely, we commit Alice Conrad into the hands of Almighty God, knowing that she has gone from this life to the eternal life, where she will dwell with the God who loves her and created her. She is free of her suffering and her pain.

Gracious God, as we come to this moment of saying goodbye to Alice Conrad may we remember that you are here with us to strengthen us and hold us up. We pray that you will surround the whole family with your love and grace. Be especially close to David and the grandchildren. May they feel the continuous embrace of your love as they walk through the valley of the shadow of death. Open their eyes to the abundant life and the life everlasting that we have through Christ, our Lord. May they lean upon you for strength and help and may they have the assurance that death is not the end, but the beginning of a new and abundant life through Christ, our Lord we pray. Amen.

13.

A Homily

for

Mrs. Inez Snow
(At Christmas Time)

"Do not be afraid. For see — I am bringing you good news of
great joy for all the people. For to you is born this day in the city
of David a Savior, who is the Messiah, the Lord."
Luke 2:10

As we come to this moment of grief, we acknowledge that for many this is a happy, joyous time because it is Christmas. For us, it is a sad time because death has come into our lives at this normally happy time. However, let us allow the message of this Christmas season to speak to us in this moment. Surely there is a message of good news that can speak to us in the midst of our sadness.

A TIME OF REFLECTION

First, Christmas causes us to pause and reflect. At Christmas time, we slow down and think more about family and friends, and the love we share. So in this Christmas season, we pause now and reflect on the life of Inez Snow. We know the love she had for her family. She loved Tom, Jane, four grandchildren and three great-grandchildren. She was married for forty-two years. After her husband's death, she learned to manage the family affairs. She became a survivor — in the best sense of that word. She was a homemaker. She devoted her time to her children — supporting them at home, in school and church, and on field trips. She played the piano in various departments in Sunday School at First Baptist Church, for Fun & Fellowship, and at the Carrolton Nursing Home. She was self-taught — she heard a number and then could play it by ear. She was a great motivator. She inspired both children to go to college and to reach for the best. She loved to sew and was a good seamstress. She made June's clothes and Frank's shirts.

She was a member of First Baptist Church for over fifty years. Today, we pause and celebrate her 91 years — good and difficult, joyous and sad, victories and defeats, good health and bad. We remember her good life and thank God for her love and devotion. We remember her good life and the lives that she has touched.

GOD WITH US

Second, the Christmas season reminds us of the Emmanuel — God's promise — "God with us." God is now with you in the midst of your grief. You are not alone. You do not bear the grief by yourself. You have family, friends, your church, and community. But, most importantly, you know God is present with you. That is the wonderful promise of Christmas. We never have to bear any load completely alone. The one who is the Good Shepherd, the Emmanuel, is there with you. You know that her pain and suffering are over. We can rejoice in her lengthy life and the knowledge that she is now with the God she loved.

We know that shepherds came to Bethlehem at Christmas. The shepherds remind us of Jesus Christ, who is the Good Shepherd. The Good Shepherd is there with you to support you in your grief. The Lord is our Shepherd, and we know that he will continue to support us. Jane and Tom were loving and caring for Inez during her illness. They reached out to her and gave her support, love and attention during her time of illness. No one could ask for more than what they gave her during this time.

Ann Weems has written a Christmas poem that reminds us that God is present with us on the darkest of days.

TOWARD THE LIGHT
Too often our answer to the darkness
    Is not running toward Bethlehem
        But running away.
We ought to know by now that we can't see
    Where we're going in the dark.
Running away is rampant…
    Separation is stylish:
        Separation from mates, from friends, from self.
Run and tranquilize,
    Don't talk about it,
        Avoid.

Run away and join the army
  Of those who have already run away.
When are we going to learn that Christmas Peace
  Comes only when we turn and face the darkness?
Only then will we be able to see
  The Light of the World.[9]

Remember that God is there with you on the darkest of days. God is there with you in your grief, and God will bear you up and give you strength. God will give you light in the midst of your darkness. Be encouraged by knowing that God is present.

GOOD NEWS IN THE TIME OF BAD NEWS

Third, Christmas is good news in the midst of bad news. Mary and Joseph had a difficult time according to the Christmas story. They had to make a difficult journey to Bethlehem when Mary was expecting a child. Herod was seeking the child so he could put him to death. Israel was in slavery to the Roman empire during this time. But, in the midst of all of this great sadness, difficulty and bad news, God came with the wonderful good news of the incarnation.

In the midst of your grief there comes the assurance that death is not the end. There is birth from this world to the next. Death opens the door here, so that we might enter into the spiritual realm. Jesus said, "Because I live you shall live also," "I have come that you might have life and have it more abundantly." Inez has now gone to join her husband, Thomas, who died many years ago. We know that one day we will all pass through the doorway to the life beyond. We have the assurance that this life, however, is not the end. But that life goes on in the eternal realm.

One of Inez's favorite hymns was "The Old Rugged Cross." Let these words give us comfort.

---

9   Ann Weems, *Kneeling at Bethlehem* (Philadelphia: Westminster Press, 1987), 21.

On a hill far away stood an old rugged cross
The emblem of suffering and shame
And I love that old cross where the dearest and best
For a world of lost sinners was slain
To the old rugged cross I will ever be true
It's shame and reproach gladly bear
Then He will call me some day to my home far away
Where His glory forever I'll share
So I'll cherish the old rugged cross
Til my trophies at last I lay down.[10]

We cling to that hope and promise today. God's love has indeed redeemed us.

One of my favorite hymns at Christmas time was written by Phillips Brooks. He penned these words:

O Holy child of Bethlehem
Descend to us, we pray
Cast out our sin and enter in
Be born in us today

We hear the Christmas angels
The great glad tidings tell
O come to us, abide with us
Our Lord, Emmanuel[11]

Listen in the midst of your sorrow to hear the angelic voices — the voice of God. God comes on the darkest of days to let us know that he is present. In this Christmas season in the midst of your grief, remember that we celebrate the birth of the Emmanuel.

---

10 Don Hustad, editor. "On a Hill Far Away," *Hymns for the Living Church* (Carol Stream, Illinois: Hope Publishing Company, 1974), 236.

11 Phillips Brooks, "O Little Town of Bethlehem," Hustad, *Hymns for the Living Church*, 121.

God is with you to strengthen you, encourage you, and to sustain you. May you sense God's love and grace. Let us pray.

Heavenly Father, we pray now that You will bind this family up in the arms of Your love. May Jane and Tom sense Your supportive presence. May the assurance of life everlasting through Jesus Christ give to us comfort and strength in the days ahead as we lean upon the One who is the Emmanuel — God with us. Amen.

A Homily

for

Leslie Myrtle
(A Long Life)

"To See the Stars"

Psalm 136:7-9

The scriptures tell us that "God made the moon and the stars to rule by night but his love endures forever."

As two small children came in the front door as it was beginning to get dark, one turned to the other and said, "Do you know that you can't see the stars until it gets dark?" Well, of course that's true but the stars are shining all the time. Only the darkness reveals them.

Today we gather in the midst of the darkness of grief as we mourn the loss of this good woman. Yet we know that the stars are continuing to shine even in the light of this day. Let me offer to you some stars which may give you guidance along your path of grief.

THE STAR OF HOPE

Paul has reminded us, "Now abideth faith, hope and love." In the time of grief and sorrow we need a sense of hope. God is present with us. Our hope is that the grave is not the end but that life continues. We cling to that strong hope today.

When I was a young minister, I was preaching once in a church in the mountains. As I was driving to the church, I got into a heavy fog. As I drove along, there were times I could hardly see the road at all. I wondered if I was going to be able to make it. Suddenly, as I got to the top of a hill, the fog cleared and the sunlight came into the car and filled it with all of its radiance and beauty and then I disappeared into the fog again. The awareness came to me so clearly. The sun is always shining, whether the fog obscures it or not. So now in this moment remember that the sunshine and starlight of God's presence is with you. God is here, even when you do not know it or feel it. God is here. Cling to that strong hope.

THE STAR OF MEMORY

Mrs. Myrtle was born in Columbus County, 91 years ago. She was married to Clarence Myrtle for fifty years. She was the mother of seven sons and one daughter. Three sons died earlier in her life. She is survived by eighteen grandchildren, twenty-three great-grandchildren, and seven great-great-grandchildren.

She was a special woman who had a deep faith and strong spirit. She was able to live in her home by herself until she went to the hospital just a few days ago. She had great powers of endurance. The family said that she was tough in discipline. But she had always exercised this discipline with a smile and love. She reminded them, "You'll do what I want while you live in my home."

A policeman asked her one day the secret she had for bringing up so many boys. Their father owned a blacksmith shop and she said the boys had only so much time to get home from school. Then as each got home they always had some task to do. They all had a job. They had no free time for mischief.

Mrs. Myrtle always encouraged her family to "smile no matter how bad the day." They all had great love and respect for her. She always loved and worked with her family. She would listen to them. Any time someone in the family would want to talk with her, she would always put on the coffee pot and they could sit down and talk. They felt like when they left they had been helped and they always felt better.

This good woman taught her family many important lessons. One of these was tough love through discipline. Another was if you don't respect yourself nobody else will. To little Danny, she used to say, and others have learned to see it as a lesson for them too, "You want what you want when you want it. When you get what you want, you don't want what you get. So want what you want when you want it." This was a very valuable lesson in trying to teach them to set their priorities early in life's journey.

She also taught them what love is. She used to say, "Love is something sent down from heaven and motivates the heck out of you. You've got to work at it every day." You could not take love for granted, you always had to show and express it. She said always remember John 3:16, "For God so loved the world that God gave his only begotten son that whosoever believes in him would not perish but have everlasting life." This is the great testimony of our faith. She encouraged the family members to live by it.

I think the following poem entitled, "Keep a Goin'" expresses something about her philosophy of life.

> If you strike a thorn or rose,
>   Keep a Goin'!
> If it hails or if it snows,
>   Keep a Goin'!
> Taint no use to sit an' whine
> When the fish ain't on the line
> Bait your hook an' keep a tryin'
>   Keep a Goin'.
>
> When the weather kills your crop,
>   Keep a Goin'
> Though 'tis work to reach the top
>   Keep a Goin'
> S'pose you're out o' ev'ry dime
> Gitten broke ain't any crime;
> Tell the world you're feelin' prime-
>   Keep a Goin'
>
> When it looks like all is up,
>   Keep a Goin'
> Drain the sweetness form the cup
>   Keep a Goin'
> See the wild birds on the wing
> Hear the bells that sweetly ring
> When you feel like sighen, sing-
>   Keep a Goin'![12]

---

12   L. L. Perry, Wrightmann F. Melton & M. D. Collins *Frank Lebby Stanton: Georgia's First Port Laureate* (Atlanta, Georgia State Department of Education, 1938), 6.

STAR OF COMFORT

We weep today but we do not weep as those who have no hope. We know that it is okay to express our grief. But we rejoice in the many good years that we had with this good woman. Remember that the word, "comfort" comes from two Latin words, "*Con fortes*" which means "with strength." We find strength from God's presence to bear us through this grief.

We know that we are not alone. We have God's presence. Christ is the Good Shepherd here with us, and he will bear us up. We also have the comfort of family and friends to let us know that we don't face the death of our mother, grandmother and friend alone.

THE STAR OF JESUS CHRIST

Revelation 22:16 states, "I am the bright and morning star." In Jesus Christ we have seen what God is like. God is love and compassion and concern, tenderness and grace. Jesus Christ has given to us the assurance of life everlasting. We come to this moment of separation affirming that death is not the end but it is a new beginning. It is a doorway that opens from this life to a new eternal life. We walk through the valley of the shadow of death with Christ's presence with us. Today we affirm that death is a birthing from this life—this physical life—to the spiritual life God has prepared for us.

We often hold hands to affirm our tenderness and love. We shake hands to greet one another because of friendship. Today, place your hand in the hand of Christ. Do not be frightened of the darkness. Know that Christ is present with you. Jesus said, "I will not leave you comfortless. I have gone to prepare a place for you." Today we rest in the assurance that Jesus Christ has taken this good woman by the hand from this life to the eternal realm which God has prepared. This good woman, who lived her life in faith and trust, has now died in faith and she has gone to that eternal home which God has prepared.

John Greenleaf Whittier has given us a poem which in many ways we might ascribe to Mrs. Myrtle. Listen to the words of this poem.

> For all her quiet life flowed on
> As meadow streamlets flow.
> Where fresher green reveals alone
> The noiseless ways they go.
>
> Her path shall brighten more and more
> Unto the perfect day;
> She cannot fail of peace who bore
> Such peace with her away.
>
> How reverent in our midst she stood,
> Or knelt in grateful praise!
> What grace of Christian womanhood
> Was in her household ways!

For still her holy living meant
No duty felt undone;
The heavenly and the human bent
Their kindred loves in one.

The dear Lord's best interpreters
Are humble human souls;
The Gospel of a life like hers
Is more than books or scrolls.[13]

O God of Love, we thank you for the life of this good woman, Leslie Myrtle. We thank you for the assurance today that she now shares in the eternal life which you have prepared. Surround all of the family the sons and daughter, the grandchildren, the great grandchildren, the great-great

---

13 John Greenleaf Whittier, "From the Friend's Burial," Morrison, *Masterpieces of Religious Verse*, 392.

grandchildren and friends with the arms of your love. May the embrace of your presence give them comfort and strength and may they lean upon you knowing that you are there with them as the Good Shepherd. As we pray in the name of Christ our Lord. Amen.

15.

A Homily

for

Jessie Humphrey

(A School Teacher for 41 Years)

Genesis 5:1

The Bible is filled with many references to books. It refers to books of prophecy, the book of generations, books of law, the book of Moses, the book of life, and others. Jessie was a teacher and knew the value of books. Let us pause today and see if certain books might not help us as we journey through our time of grief.

THE BOOK OF KNOWLEDGE

Jessie was a teacher and books were a part of her education, what she used in the education of others, and her family. Jessie was a school teacher for forty-one years. She taught at Smith, Barker Ten Mile, and Lumberton City Schools. Like her Lord, Jessie was a teacher. She wanted her teaching time to be very productive. She touched the lives of many people. She probably influenced at least three generations of students and parents. Her family members said, often someone would meet her in the store and comment that she had been their teacher. Her own children were challenged by Jessie to continue pursuing their own education as far as they possibly could. Jessie was, indeed, a person who drew on the book of knowledge.

THE BOOK OF REMEMBRANCE.

In the quietness of this moment, we reflect on Jessie's good, productive, and useful life. She was not only a teacher, but a good example of a working mom. She not only taught school, but ran the home. She and Charles gave to their children a wonderful model of what a good marriage and family were like. They were married sixty-two and one-half years. Their children said they never heard a quarrel or that they never had a cross word. At least, they never heard them. They were devoted and loving to each other and to their family. Jessie and Charles were a loving and devoted husband and wife. They were always together.

Jessie provided strength, order, and stability to her family. Dinner was always on time. They knew to be present and not to be late. She gave them the feeling that the world was orderly and that home was a safe and secure place. Jessie also pushed and challenged her children to be their best, without saying what that had to be. She encouraged them to be who they could be and helped them to know who they were. She affirmed and appreciated them. They had a sense of security in knowing they could ask her for help and guidance. She could also be firm, though. She told one of her daughters, when she was a teenager, "You cannot go out until your room is clean." Jessie taught her children good work ethics. She imparted values of education and doing one's best. "Whatever you can do, do it well," she told them. She did not dictate, but guided.

Jessie also supported Charles when he was Mayor and had to make hard decisions. There would be times when he could not sleep, and would be rolling and tossing. She would ask him, "Do you think you are doing the right thing?" "Yes," he would say. Then Jessie would respond, "Okay, turn over and go to sleep!" Jessie and Charles did a lot of traveling after they both retired. They enjoyed their trips and their special times together. Jessie also delivered church literature to the shut-ins until just recently. Often, she would go for visits to Hermitage and was at Wesley Pines every Monday.

Jessie had a high appreciation for fine clothes and liked to dress nicely. She thought that it was important to look well, as to know many things. Today, we continue to remember the love that she had for Charles, and he for her, and that they shared for their three children and six grandchildren. Today, we remember Charlie's loving care and devoted attention to her during her illness and declining years. No one could have been more loving or attentive.

BOOK OF FAITH

Jessie was a dedicated Christian woman. Her father was a Baptist minister and she was steeped in the Baptist tradition. She loved her Lord, her church, and was faithful in attendance on Sunday and Wednesday. She taught a Sunday School class for forty years. For thirteen years she and Charles worked in the BTU with thirteen year olds. Imagine, thirteen years with thirteen year olds! One of the best memories family members said they had of her was seeing her sitting and reading. She often read her Bible and other materials, especially materials from Billy Graham. She loved to listen to Billy Graham and watch his program.

One of Jessie's greatest gifts to her family was her commitment to God. She passed on high values, and the knowledge of right and wrong. She had a strong faith and trust in God, even during her illness and declining years. She affirmed God's presence with her. So today, like Jessie, we trust God and lean back in our faith upon God.

BOOK OF LIFE

Jesus said, "I am the resurrection and the life." Death is not the end; it is a beginning of a new chapter. The night before Jessie died, she prayed for her whole family by name. She prayed for Charles, her children, her grandchildren, and others. She seemed to know that the end was near. She wanted to remember them in a very special way. What a wonderful evidence of a strong faith. Her physical body is dead, but now she has a spiritual body. This is a new beginning. Jesus said, "I have gone to prepare a place for you." Her death is a birthing from this life to the next life. For the Christian, death is not the end, but the beginning of a new and wonderful life.

Billy Graham was one of Jessie's favorite preachers. In his autobiography entitled, *Just As I Am*, Billy Graham concluded his book with some beautiful lines. To me, they are symbolic; not only for Billy Graham, but reflect very strongly the life of Jessie, as well.

But I look forward to Heaven.
I look forward to the reunion with friends and loved ones who have gone on before.
I look forward to Heaven's freedom from sorrow and pain.

I also look forward to serving God in ways we can't begin
to imagine, for the Bible makes it clear that Heaven is not a
place of idleness.
And most of all, I look forward to seeing Christ and bowing
before Him in praise and gratitude for all He has done for us,
and for using me on this earth by His grace — just as I am.[14]

Now at her time of death, Jessie has placed her hand quietly
in the hand of Christ, to move from this life to the next. She has
walked through that dark valley to the land of light and joy. She is
now free of her pain and suffering. She has begun a new chapter
in the Lamb's book of life. In our church we traditionally grant
letters of transfer to persons when they move from one church to
another. So today, we grant to Jessie her transfer of letter from the
church mortal to the church immortal, from the physical church
to the spiritual church, where she has gone to dwell eternally with
the God she loves.

In one of the favorite books that Jessie had for devotional
reading, there are some lines from Helen Steiner Rice. These lines
seem appropriate as we reflect on the life of Jessie today.

> When I must leave you
> for a little while,
> Please do not grieve
> and shed wild tears
> And hug your sorrow
> to you through the years,
> But start out bravely
> with a gallant smile;
> And for my sake
> and in my name
> Live on and do
> all things the same,

---

14 Billy Graham, *Just As I Am: The Autobiography of Billy Graham* (San Fran-
cisco: Harper Collins, 1997), 730.

Feed not your loneliness,
　　on empty days,
But fill each waking hour
　　in useful ways,
Reach out your hand
　　in comfort and in cheer
And I in turn will comfort you
　　and hold you near;
And never, never
　　be afraid to die,
For I am waiting
　　for you in the sky![15]

God of Grace, we thank You for the good life of Jessie Humphrey, and for the love she shared with Charles, Bill, Tony, Catherine, her sisters, six grandchildren, and all of her other friends. Surround Charles, the children, and all of her other loved ones with Your grace and assurance. Give to them, this moment, the awareness that You are with them and that Jessie shares in that eternal life that you have prepared. Now may the grace, comfort, and love of God the Father, Son, and Holy Spirit sustain you both now and forever more. Amen.

15　Helen Steiner Rice, "When I Must Leave You," Rice, *Just for Me,* 39.

16.

A HOMILY

FOR

JACK DANIEL NYE
(A BUSINESS MAN)

JOHN 14:1-7

John Watson, a noted Scottish preacher, used to go and lean over and whisper in the ear of one of his dying church members these words, "In my father's house are many mansions." He said the Christian would then slip away, quietly and unafraid, into God's hands.

Today, we come to these moments as we reflect on the life of Jack Nye. Let us draw upon the words of Jesus from the fourteenth chapter of John for comfort.

Unafraid of the Future

First, Jesus said, "Let not your heart be troubled." Our faith in Jesus Christ dispels our fear. We know we can lean on God as Jesus told us. He told his disciples not to worry about the future. And so, today in quiet faith, we rest on God. Today, our hearts are not troubled, because we lean in quiet trust in the confidence and assurance of life everlasting through Jesus Christ, our Lord.

Reflecting on a Good Life

We remember also, today, the good quality of Jack's life. Jack was a native of Robeson County and was born seventy-seven years ago. Jack was an active businessman, who owned Jack Nye's TV Service Center. He was noted as an excellent television repairman. Jack was an active member of First Baptist Church and attended faithfully the Men's Fellowship Sunday School class. He was a Mason and also a Shriner. He was a lifetime member of the Lions Club and was voted Lion of the Year. As a World War II veteran, Jack served in the Army Air Corps. He was married to Lois for almost fifty years. They were devoted to each other.

Jack is remembered as a kind and gentle spirit. He was, indeed, a gentle man — a gentleman. Family members said they remember his deep love and personal concern for others. He helped hold the family together. He was a positive, affirmative person — always gracious and cheerful. He loved to talk and he loved to be around people. We shall miss his wonderful spirit. He was devoted to Mary Lois, her mother, Chuck and his family. "Uncle Jack", as he was called, had an impact for good on three generations as they knew and experienced his love and unselfish attitude.

BELIEVE IN GOD

Jesus told us that we are also to believe in God. So today, we lean back in quiet faith in God, knowing that we do not face death alone, but underneath are the everlasting arms. God is there to sustain us. So like a small child, we reach up and place our hand in the hand of God, and trust in the everlasting goodness of God. Jesus has revealed to us what God is like. God is a God of love, grace, concern and care. Jesus is the Good Shepherd who cares for each of us and today we know He is concerned about us and the grief that we bear.

JACK'S HOME-GOING

Reflect on the words from Jesus, "In my father's house are many mansions." Today, we acknowledge Jack's home-going. He is gone to that place Christ has prepared for all those who love him. It is a place where there is rest and no suffering, where there is joy and peace. Jesus has assured us that this place is there. He said, "If it were not so, I would have told you." Today, the flowers represent not only the love of the family and friends, but the resurrection garden. Because Jesus lives, we, too, shall live. There is a homing instinct within all of us that calls us back to God. In the heavenly home we will know each other there as we have been known here.

PEACE OF JESUS

Jesus said, "My peace I leave with you." The peace of Jesus Christ gives us inner strength. His peace sustains us. We reach out quietly today to draw upon the power of Christ's presence. Our strength is not enough to bear our grief, but His strength gives us the ability to bear the load of grief and to look to the future with hope.

PREPARING A PLACE

Jesus said, "I have gone to prepare a place for you." This will be a place where there is rest from our labor and freedom from our difficulties and pain. As Christians, we affirm that death is not a wall, but a door. Death is not a dead end, but a new path to God. Death is not an end, but a new beginning. "Because I live," Jesus said, "you shall live also."

Some years ago on a trip to Switzerland, a traveler was uncertain of the way to drive to Kandersteg. He asked a small lad standing by the roadside where Kandersteg was. The traveler was surprised by the lad's answer. "I don't know, sir," the lad responded, but there is the road to it." None of us has been to the Celestial City, but Jesus has pointed the way for us. When we pass through the doorway of death, we enter into a new dimension where we are with our Master. We know that will be a good place because our Lord is there. We will sense His love, compassion, and grace. We follow down this road by faith to the place Christ has gone to prepare for us.

Today we affirm that Jack has left this earthly place to be with the God he loves and shares in the eternal life that all Christians are promised. Let us pray.

Loving Father, we thank You for Jack Nye, for the good life of this gentle and kind man. We thank You for the assurance that he now shares eternally in the home that You have prepared. Surround Mary Lois and his family and friends today with the strength of Your love. May we leave this place comforted to serve and love You better. Through Christ, our Lord, we pray. Amen

A Homily

for

Milton Lee Torrance
(A Gentle Man)

"Peace Within"

John 14:27

P eace brings to our minds different images, doesn't it?

-A soft breeze on your face as you walk along the beach watching the waves break on the shore.
-Working in your beautiful flower garden
-Watching a tiny baby sleep at night
-Sitting by a warm fire on a cold winter night
-Walking in the mountains in the fall of the year
-Watching the sun rise over your favorite lake
-Holding a loved one in your arms
-Sitting around the Christmas tree or around the table for Christmas dinner.

All these things are signs of human peace. But Jesus offers "a peace that passes all understanding." This peace is not dependent on external factors. It gives us inner stability in the midst of the storms and difficulties of life. It is a peace that no one can take away from us when we have it within. Milton's favorite verse was John 14:27- "Peace I leave you, my peace I give unto you, not as the world gives, give I unto you." Let's examine this verse briefly as we reflect on the life of Milton and the strength it can give us for our grief and affirm our faith.

THE SOURCE OF THIS PEACE

Jesus offered to his disciples this peace in his departing words to them, "I give to you." His peace is inseparable from his presence. Jesus is the author of this peace. This peace had enabled Jesus to face ridicule, rejection, discouragement, misunderstanding, suffering, and death. In obedience to his father's will and in sacrificial devotion to ushering in the Kingdom of God, Jesus reflected an inner calm that came from his special relationship to his father. He was one with the father. Milton felt this oneness with Christ. In that union with Christ, he experienced peace.

PEACE IS CHRIST'S GIFT

The word peace was often on the lips of Jesus, "Go in Peace," or "Peace be with you." Paul often used this expression at the beginning and conclusion of many of his letters. Paul declared that, "the peace of God which passes all understanding, shall keep your hearts and minds through Christ Jesus." (Philippians 4:7). Christ bestows this peace upon us by bringing us into union with Christ. As we commit our life and trust Christ, he draws us to himself and reduces our

> turmoil- with calm
> our uneasiness- with security
> our noisy nature- with quietness
> our grief – with comfort

Christ is the giver himself of this peace. We acknowledge that we do not always feel at peace. Sometimes the world crowds it out. At times you can sense it and it sustains you. Milton in his time of need sensed this inner peace.

MILTON WAS AT PEACE WITH HIMSELF

Many people are not at peace with themselves. They are pulled in different directions and feel as though they would fly apart. They are unsure of who they are and hide behind masks. But I believe that Milton knew who he was and was at peace with himself.

1.   Milton was peaceful by nature
Milton never raised his voice and had a very calm spirit. The family acknowledged what a wonderful listener he was. You could talk to him at any time. He would ask, "How are you?" and he really meant it. He was a compassionate, caring, listening person.

2.   He lived peaceably with others.

He always looked for good in others and taught his children to respect all people. He saw good values in others. He was kind and good to all persons. He said to his children, "If you can't say anything nice, don't say it. We never know," he said, "what's going on in another person's life. They may be experiencing hard times, a bad day or an illness." Milton, Jr. said that his mother told him one time that he was too much like his dad and that he might get hurt. Then she added, "That's okay, it's a good way to go through life." Milton considered it a high compliment to be compared to his father.

3.   Milton had a wonderful peace with his own family.

He had a deep love and devotion to Emma. She and Milton had a very sweet and thoughtful relationship to each other. They still held hands like young love-birds. They were married for 55 years, had 2 children, 6 grandchildren and one-great grandchild called "Jumpy-Jumpy." Milton was PaPa to his grandchildren.

Milton always gave special interest and attention to his children. He would always travel on his job and try to be home by Thursday to be with his family. He supported the children in whatever they wanted to do in school, music and sports. The children always felt comfortable bringing their friends home. Their friends enjoyed being there. Milton loved to cook breakfast for the family. He would always sing to wake the children and grandchildren up. "Good morning, good morning," he sang, "How are you this morning? - Nobody loves me, I'll eat some worms."

He wanted his children to have a good education. They went to Baptist colleges, Meredith and Wake Forest. He told them to do the best they could and to work hard. He had a way of helping them overcome their homesickness. He would always say, "Stay one night, and if you don't like it, I'll come get you." He knew if they stayed one night they would like it.

The grandchildren called him "Papa." They said he was the kindest, most honest man they ever knew. They wanted to live like he did and be like he would want them to be. He had a great influence on the grandchildren. One of them said to Milton, "You've always been a great inspiration to me. I always looked up to you."

He and Emma would often come to Jane's house and stay a week or three weeks with the children. He would fish and fix them meals and they would always enjoy these times together. He had math games that he played with them, and they became aware of his great mathematical skills. He taught them how to do these games as well. At the mountain cabin he and the children and grandchildren had given special names to places, trees and other objects there.

4. Humor

Milton was fun to be with. He made life fun. He would make a game even of cleaning up. He loved good jokes. Red Skelton was his model. One time he had a friend who wanted to be in a golf tournament but he was not a very good golfer. Milton asked if they would let him and his friend tee off from the ladies' tee. The sponsors said only if he wore a skirt. The day of the tournament, the crowd saw these two ugly women coming up the path with skirts on. Milton and his friend had dressed up like women and wore wigs and skirts and played golf that way. Everybody had a great laugh and delight in it. This was another expression of his wonderful sense of humor.

5. Golf

Milton loved to play golf. He took a limb at the mountain cabin and carved it and sanded it so he could practice his golf there in the mountains.

PEACE WITH GOD

Milton taught his children about God and took them to Sunday School and Worship. They used to sit in the balcony because that was where the children wanted to sit. He was not a man to verbalize his faith, but he lived it. He was honest and straightforward in everything he did.

Milton faced his illness with courage. He fought hard and never complained. His family often did not know if he was hurting or not. Someone said Milton's suffering seemed so unfair. We know that God did not send this suffering upon Milton. It is a part of life. But the family said we need to learn from Milton and take his strength with us. Milton knew that nothing separated him from God.

Just as a small child will reach up its hand and place it in the hand of its father or mother to receive comfort and strength from them, so Milton placed his hand in the hand of Christ to feel his strength and companionship through this time of suffering.

PEACE FOR THE LAST JOURNEY

Milton waited patiently when God wanted him to come home. He was a man who knew how to wait. Often when a family member would call and ask if they were going to the mountains, Milton would say that when Emma is ready, we will leave. He was waiting for Emma to tell him when she was ready to go. He would be all set but he patiently waited for her. So in this time of his illness, we know that he patiently waited for God's time of his departure.

Today we affirm that nothing separates us from the love of God. So we know that not even death can separate Milton from God's presence. We accept Christ's promise that he has gone to prepare a place for us. Jesus said that he is the resurrection and the life. Today we know that Milton is free from his suffering and pain and has taken this last journey to be with God where there is joy and peace.

The peace that Jesus gives is not as the world gives. It is inner peace. It is a peace that equips us to face any and everything that comes. It is not determined by physical surroundings but by the presence and power of God within. Jesus said, "let not the heart be troubled or afraid." So today, quietly, we trust in God.

Milton used to sit on the porch at the cabin and call to the hummingbirds. They would come to him and he would feed them. I can imagine that in that the Celestial City that Milton is now sitting, resting and feeding the beautiful birds that fly in God's Mansions of Glory.

Milton loved to go to his mountain cabin. He loved the mountains and enjoyed them so much. Picture today a stormy, snowy night. The mountains are covered in snow. Milton is down the mountain a piece from the cabin. At first he is not sure where he is but then the door of the cabin is opened and light from the cabin sends a pathway of light all the way down to where he is. He walks in that pathway of light toward his cabin. He continues to walk in the light because he knows there is warmth, comfort and companionship in the "cabin" at the end of the path of light.

Today, we acknowledge that Milton has stepped into that path of light and has walked toward the heavenly home with the companionship of our Lord. He has gone to that Celestial City and in the time of year where there is great rejoicing and celebration at the birth of the Prince of Peace. We know that Milton is now at peace. May the peace of God abide in your hearts and comfort you.

> Peace, perfect peace in this dark world of sin?
> The blood of Jesus whispers peace within.
>
> Peace, perfect peace, by thronging duties pressed?
> To do the will of Jesus, this is rest.
>
> Peace, perfect peace, with sorrows surging round?
> On Jesus' bosom naught but calm is found.
>
> > Peace, perfect peace, our future all unknown?
> > Jesus, we know and he is on the throne.
> >
> > Peace, perfect peace, death shadowing us and ours?
> > Jesus has vanquished death and all its powers.

It is enough: earth's struggles soon shall cease,
And Jesus call us to heaven's perfect peace.[16]

Let us pray.

*May the peace, comfort and joy of Christ our Lord sus-
tain you. May the peace of the one whose birth we celebrate
as the Prince of Peace comfort, direct, guide and sustain you
both now and forever more. Amen.*

---

16   "Peace, Perfect Peace," Hustad, *Hymns of the Living Church.* 396-397.

18.

A Homily
FOR
Walt Wallace Towns
(Retired Military Person)

Ephesians 6:10-17

Walt loved the military and served on active duty for many years and then was in the Air Force Reserve, finally retiring as a lieutenant colonel. In World War II he was a bomber pilot in Italy and flew seventy-two missions. He loved flying. The military was an important part of his life and it seems appropriate today to draw from the apostle Paul's military image from Ephesians 6, for some resources for our grief. Paul depicts the equipment that soldiers wore and drew spiritual truths from them. Let us see if they cannot offer us some comfort today.

THE BELT OF TRUTH

The belt that the soldier wore in Paul's day was a wide belt around the waist. It gave the soldier support and also served to as a place to hang some of his weapons. When we come to this moment we realize that Jesus Christ is the Belt of Truth. He is the one who said, "I am the way, the truth and the life." We lean upon Christ to find a sense of support and encouragement during our time of grief.

Walt had related himself to the one who was the truth and he was a man known for his honesty and truthfulness in his personal life and in his business life. He served as manager of Sherwin Williams for many years. The people trusted him and turned to him for support and guidance through the years. There was nothing inconsistent with his life and his strong Christian convictions. He followed the truth he had seen in Christ both in character and in all that he sought to do.

THE BREASTPLATE OF RIGHTEOUSNESS

The breastplate was that piece of equipment which protected the large upper body. It stood for a right relationship with God and others. Walt was a man whose life was reflected by his righteous walk. He was who he said he was. He was hard-working and was noted as a man of integrity. He was considered a paint and art expert through his work at Sherwin Williams. Many turned to him for help and guidance in this area.

Walt was always a person who was helpful. He took care of others. In his community work, he was especially active in the Lions Club. He loved their goals and ideals. He was affirmed and appreciated by those in that civic work. Walt was known for the goodness of his life.

THE SANDALS OF READINESS FOR PEACE

In the military life, a soldier often had to be willing to move quickly and often. The apostle Paul said, "I have fought the good fight." He was ready for this life and beyond. So was Walt. He had prepared his own funeral arrangements and he was ready to depart. He knew that no one ever knew when we might have to leave this life to go to the next. He trusted God whether he lived or died.

He served in the military and was a person who helped to maintain peace around the world. He leaned upon the strength that he could draw from the One who was the prince of peace. We seek to draw upon the strength of Christ today that he might give us peace in the midst of our grief.

THE SHIELD OF FAITH

The shield of Faith which Paul mentions here was as big as a door. It offered the soldier one of his greatest senses of strength and protection. So for the Christian, we live out our lives by faith and we die by faith. Faith is the marvelous shield that gives us protection and strength to face life and death.

Today we trust Christ, who has gone to prepare a place for us. We know that he has gone to prepare a place for Walt and we rest in the assurance that his struggles and difficulties are over and he is at peace with God.

Faith is the strong bridge which reaches over the valley of death. It is the bridge that carries the Christian from this life to the next life. So today we lean in quiet strength upon God for our comfort. We know that we can trust God completely and lean upon God's presence to help us get through this grief. We know that we can use the strength of God to help us walk through the valley of the shadow of death.

THE HELMET OF SALVATION

Paul knew that it was not by works of righteousness or anything we did, but redemption is by God's grace. We come now to the moment of death in which we let Walt go from this life to the next. We know there is nothing that he has done or we can do to earn salvation but in quiet trust he has leaned back on God and left this life to dwell eternally with God, who gives life and redeems us.

We know that we are sad at Walt's sudden departure. And it's okay to cry. Walt left us much too quickly and that leaves a real vacuum. Nevertheless, we are thankful for God's redemption and for the assurance that we are not alone. God is present to sustain us and carry us through our grief.

THE SWORD OF THE SPIRIT WHICH IS THE WORD OF GOD

For the Christian, prayer is that sword that gives us strength to go through whatever trials we bear in life. As we face the valley of the shadow of death we know that we can depend on God. Our Lord has gone to prepare a place for us. We know that we are not alone in our grief but the Lord is with us.

As Christians we affirm that death is not the end. It is a birth from this life to the next life, for the Christian. We know that Walt has passed from this earthly life to his heavenly life. The mortal flesh has put on immortality. The physical has put on the spiritual. He has gone through the transition of a birth from this life to the next.

When J. B. Phillips, who later became a noted translator of the New Testament, was a young minister in Penge outside of London, he almost died from peritonitis. The surgeon who removed his appendix did not think he would live through the night. While he was asleep, Phillips had a dream where he saw himself alone, depressed and miserable as he trudged down a dusty slope. Along his pathway he saw ruined houses, stagnant water, rusty tin cans and rubbish of all kinds. As he travelled downward, he looked up and saw on the other side of the valley a home of indescribable beauty. As he approached the stream below, he was surrounded by mountains, streams, forests, clouds and birds singing. As he raced down the hill toward the beautiful house his heart was filled with joy. He saw a shiny white bridge across the stream and he ran toward it. As he reached the bridge, a figure dressed in white appeared and smiling gestured for him to return up the dreary slope. He said he had never felt such disappointment as he began to walk back up the hill and he burst into tears. Suddenly he awoke from his dream and found himself weeping. The nurse on duty asked him why he was weeping because "you're going to live." Later Phillips would say that dream gave him assurance of life after death and empowered him to do his effective ministry later. In the final days of his life he said that vivid dream "remains as true and clear to me today as it was then." That dream was for him a powerful assurance of life after death.

What life beyond death will be like is beyond our imagination. But what can an unborn child in his mother's womb really know about the world outside his mother's body. He or she lives without air. How can he understand what it means to breathe fresh air? She sees no light. How can she describe it? He is fed by a tube attached to his mother. How can he understand what it is like to eat food? The crisis of birth may seem like a death to him or her as he or she emerges from a secure, known world. Death is like that for us. It is a "birthing" from the physical world with which we are familiar to the unknown spiritual world. We fall asleep in this earthly life and then we awaken in the eternal realm of God's heaven where our suffering and pain are over. A new unknown world awaits us. By faith we can enter this world at peace with the God who has made us. God picks us up from the "womb" of this life and places us in the eternal home which he has prepared.

So in quietness and strength, we lean upon God. Trusting in our faith in God, we know that God is here with us. As we reflect upon Walt's life and his commitment to the military, we draw strength from these military images today. They remind us of the love and presence of God who sustains us no matter what we face in life.

Alfred Lord Tennyson in his poem entitled, "Crossing the Bar" gives us the assurance that God is present. Hear the words of this poem.

> Sunset and evening star,
>> And one clear call for me!
> And may there be no moaning of the bar
>> When I put out to sea.
> But such a tide as moving seems asleep,
>> Too full for sound or foam,
> When that which drew from out the boundless deep
>> Turns again home.
> Twilight and evening bell,
>> And after that the dark!
> And may there be no sadness of farewell
>> When I embark;
> For though from out our bourne of time and place
>> The flood may bear me far,
> I hope to see my Pilot face to face,
>> When I have crossed the bar.[17]

Eternal Father, we thank you for the assurance that we can rest in you. No matter what comes to us in life, we know are not alone. You are present to comfort and sustain us. We thank you for the good life of Walt Towns and for the assurance that he now shares in the eternal life that you have prepared for all those who love you. Encircle this family in the arms of your love. May the embrace of your presence give them courage and strength. Walk with them each step of the way in the valley of the shadows that they might see

17 Alfred Lord Tennyson, "Crossing the Bar," Morrison, *Masterpieces of Religious* Verse, 615.

the sunlight at the end and know that you will be there to guide them through. In the name of Jesus Christ, our living Lord we pray. Amen.

19.

A Homily
for
Marie Arthur
(A Homemaker)

John 14:2-3, 27

The three most honored words in the human language, I believe, are home, heaven and mother. The three are closely linked together because they are related. Jesus often used images of the home to describe the kingdom of God and our heavenly home. Home and mother are central figures to our life and religion. Today we remember Marie as a mother and homemaker. She was a dedicated mother and loving wife. She enjoyed her home and family, and devoted herself to making her home a good one. She was always busy with many things at home. She wanted to share what she had and give something to other people. She was good at sewing and cooking, and her family enjoyed the mealtimes.

She was a good neighbor and always took something to her neighbors when she visited them. She never visited with an empty hand. Marie was married to Wallace for forty-seven years, a loving wife and mother. She and her sisters were all very close; they had a loving relationship. Lillian spoke of her sister as a great, sweet sister. Marie was a quiet, easygoing, caring and dedicated person. We remember her love for her home and family.

Fear Dispelled

The words from the fourteenth chapter of John give us some sources to help us as we face our grief. First, Jesus said, "Let not your heart be troubled." Our faith in Christ dispels our fear. We lean back in quiet trust on God. Jesus assured His disciples and us, that even when our heart is troubled, God is with us. Our hearts are sad, but they are not broken. We are thankful that Marie's suffering is over and that she has gone to be with the God that she loved. We remember the loving care from Wallace, Jeffery and other family members. We know that life will be different now without her. We will miss her, but we would not want her back to suffer. Our hearts are at peace because we know that God is with us.

BELIEVE IN GOD

Second, Jesus said, "believe in God." We lean back in faith on God to know that we face our grief not alone, but the everlasting arms are underneath us and God is there to sustain us. Lou Anne told me that when Marie was a small child in the Raft Swamp Baptist Church, she used to sing so loud sometimes that her voice could be heard above others. They wanted to tell her to be quiet, but she continued to sing. She always had a song on her heart. Family members have indicated that she knew most of the hymns by heart. She and Wally used to help put out candy in Sunday School class before the members got there. She loved her church and her Sunday School class.

TRUST CHRIST

Third, Jesus said, "believe also in Me." Jesus has revealed to us what God is like. God is love, grace, concern and care. Jesus is the good shepherd who cares for us and walks with us through this grief. Just as a child lifts up its hand to put it in its father or mother's hand, for guidance through an unknown place, so today, quietly, Marie has placed her hand in the hand of Christ, to walk into that place He has prepared.

HOME-GOING

Fourth, Jesus said, "In my Father's house are many rooms." Today Marie has a home-going. She has gone to that place that Christ has prepared. Her suffering is over. She has gone to rest where there is joy and peace. Jesus has assured us that, "If this were not so, I would have told you." The flowers today symbolize not only the love of family and friends, but the resurrection garden. We know that death is not the end. There is a homing instinct in all of us that draws us to God. We know that God knows Marie, and she is there in the home that He has prepared. There is room for all.

THE PEACE OF JESUS

Fifth, Jesus said, "My peace I leave with you." The peace of Jesus gives us inner strength and His peace sustains us. We reach out now in our grief to draw upon the power of His presence. We know that our strength is not enough, but we reach out to Him. On the morning of Marie's death, some of the nurses in the nursing home said that they heard Marie singing, "Amazing Grace." Even in her suffering, she still had a sense of the presence of God and sang of God's amazing grace that sustained her.

A PREPARED PLACE

Sixth, Jesus said, "I have gone to prepare a place for you." This is a definite place where we will rest from our labors, difficulties and pain. We know that Marie is now home in this heavenly place that our Lord has provided. Death is not a wall, but a door. Death is not a dead-end, but a new pathway to God. Death is not an end, but a beginning. Jesus said, "Because I live, you shall live also." And we know today Marie has gone to be with the God that she loves.

Years ago there was a noted New England Minister, named John Todd. He received a letter from his aged aunt that she had a grave disease and was not likely to recover. Her letter was sad and mournful. Rev. Todd wrote a response to her, in which he reminded her that thirty-five years ago, when he was a boy of six, his parents had died and he had to go live with her. He was met at the train station by a black man who carried him on his horse to meet his aunt. He said, "I started for my new home and then I asked Caesar," the man who was leading him to his aunt's home, "Do you think she will go to bed before we get there?" "Oh, no!" He replied. "She will sure stay up for you. When we get out of these woods you will see a light right enough."

Presently, he said, they rode into a clearing and he saw a light in the window. He said, "I remember that you were waiting at the door and you put your arms around me and lifted me, a tired and bewildered little boy, down from the horse. There was a bright fire on the hearth, a warm supper on the stove. After supper you took me up to my room, heard me say my prayers, then sat beside me until I fell asleep." He continues, "You are probably wondering why I am recalling all of this to your mind. Someday God will send for you, to take you to your messenger of death. At the end of the road you will find love and a welcome; you will be safe in God's care and keeping. God can be trusted – trusted to be as kind to you, as you were to me, so many years ago."

Marie has passed now from this land into that land where she is met by the gracious God who loves her. He has reached out with His warmth and love to embrace her. She is met by family and friends who have gone on before her. We know that because Jesus lives, we shall live also. We give God thanks that Marie has gone to be with the God that she loves.

> *O Gracious God, we thank you for the good life of Marie Arthur. We pray now that You will put the arms of Your love around Walter, James, Emily and other family members, and may they know that You are here with them in the midst of their grief. May they be strengthened by the assurance of life everlasting through Jesus Christ. As they go through these days ahead, may they always know that nothing separates them from Your love. Now may the comfort, peace and love of Jesus Christ, God the Father and the Holy Spirit watch over and bless you, both now and forever more. Amen.*

20.

A Homily
for
Hillard W. Tuck
(The Walk of Life)

Ephesians 4:1

I heard my father say on several occasions that he had the healthiest job in the world. For thirty-five years he carried a pack on his back as he delivered mail. He walked about fourteen miles every day. Much of his life was spent in walking, so it seemed appropriate to me this afternoon to use the theme of "walk" as a symbol for his life.

The Bible often uses "walking" as a word to describe different aspects of life. In Genesis it states, "Before whom my fathers did walk" (Genesis 48:15). "Ask the good way and walk therein" (Jeremiah 6:18). Micah reminds us "walk humbly with your God" (Micah 6:8). "Walk in newness of life" (Romans 6:4). "Walk worthy of your vocation" (Ephesians 4:1); "Walk worthy of the Lord" (Colossians 1:10).

THE WALK OF LIFE

"Ask the good way and walk in it"

We pause today to remember the good walk of Hillard W. Tuck. For eighty-five years he walked the good life among us. He experienced, like all of us, good times and difficult times, happy and sad moments, joys and sorrows. But through it all he was a good man. We thank God for that. Today we express our gratitude for the years we shared with him as family and friends. But even at its longest, life is still brief. We know life will be different without him, and he will be missed. But we are thankful for the many wonderful years he walked among us.

Today he is survived by his wife, three children, nine grandchildren, sixteen great grandchildren, and one brother. He is preceded in death by one grandchild. He and mother shared sixty-four years of married life together. Few can have that long a time together. No one will ever forget the love and tender care mother has given daddy during his time of illness. No one could have been more loving and tender.

WE OBSERVED HIS WALK - THE WAY HE LIVED.

"Walk worthy of the Lord"

I learned many valuable lessons from my father as did all of the members of my family. He had a book in his room written by Leo Tolstoy entitled *What Men Live By*. I don't know whether my father ever read that book or not, but he certainly had a philosophy he lived by and which he passed on to us.

My father was always a quiet, private person. He was a hard-working man. I remember how for many years after he would deliver the mail on his regular job, at nights, afternoons, or week-ends, he would paint houses, work in his garden or always be involved in some building project. He was always busy and was not content unless he was doing something. My mother was recently notified that the post office auxiliary wanted to give my father a fifty-year pen.

He loved the outdoors and walked in it every day. One of the interesting experiences he had during this time was that he was followed by a little black dog named Flickie. Flickie would meet my father at the bus stop where Daddy would get off and begin his mail route. Every day of the week Flickie would wait there for Daddy and walk with him all around his route until Daddy had finished delivering his mail. Only then would Flickie go home. Sundays when my father did not work, Flickie would wait for the bus and after a while when Daddy didn't come, Flickie would go home. For some time, two other dogs started following Daddy. For a long time, Daddy had three dogs following him around his mail route. Every Christmas he always received a present from "Flickie."

Daddy's love of the outdoors involved him in fishing and hunting. He loved them both. Many of you here today have hunted and fished with him or he has used your land on which to do both. I have heard many people talk about what a crack shot my father was and how often he could catch a fish when no one else seemed able to do so. He took great pride in his heritage. He loved his family and was proud of his roots. He never lost touch with who he was and knew what was expected of him. As someone said, "He was a Virginia gentleman."

Daddy and mother started my sister, brother and me going to church and Sunday School when we were very small. That was important to them. Daddy was a man of strong convictions and opinions and did not hesitate to express them, whether it was about politics, religion or anything else. Sometimes he could do that in earthy language. He was strong-willed and determined to fulfill his goals and convictions. He recognized and repudiated phoniness in people -whether it was in religion, politics or in daily life. He called some preachers "religious hucksters".

He placed honesty and integrity at the top of his list and was true to his convictions and belief. He despised those who were not honest and true to their word. He believed in doing things right and would not let a bill get cold on his desk before it had to be paid. He loved sports and pitched baseball when he was in high school. He loved to watch all kinds of sports, especially baseball. When he was younger he was an excellent croquet player, almost a professional. He played on the Miller Park Croquet Court, which had a sand base. I and other members of the family, have traveled with him to Roanoke and other places to watch him and others compete in tournaments. I have seen him hit a ball at the other end of the court. He was, without question, a pro in croquet. We remember his laugh and sense of humor. He liked a good joke.

He loved his family and placed family as one of his prized values. Dad was always affectionately known as Papa. We will never forget his flat top, his pipe, his favorite chair, his strong will, and his love for his family. He had a plaque in his bedroom which was given to him from his grandchildren entitled "Worlds Greatest Grandpa Award." It reads like the following:

"You've won this well deserved title for:
Preserving the values of yesterday
To give me something to believe in today.
Teach me the importance of hard work and self-respect.

Telling me all the stories and yarns from the 'good old days'.
And for giving me someone I can always look up to - you".
The walk through the Valley of the Shadow of Death.
"Yea, though I walk through the valley of the shadow of death."

We do not walk through this dark valley alone. We have the presence of our family and friends, but especially God. We weep today - because life will be different without Daddy. And tears are O.K. We know that Jesus wept beside the grave of Lazarus. We weep today, but we weep, not as those without hope. The valley of grief is not a dead end or cul-de-sac for us, but is a pathway that leads through to a life beyond where there is peace, rest, joy and blessedness.

A neighbor, a young woman, who is a campus minister at Lynchburg College, told me and other members of the family about how often she would visit daddy in the neighborhood and later in the hospital. On one of her visits to the hospital, he told her that he was ready to go. He said he had lived a good life and had had more than many could ever ask for in life. She asked him what that was, and he said he had had the wonderful love of his wife and he was proud of his family, his children and grandchildren.

I believe that Daddy knew he would not get well. He faced his death with a Stoic, strong determination and inner faith to meet it quietly and bravely, which he did. He met death surrounded by his wife and family and the prayers of many others.

HIS WALK DOES NOT END WITH THIS LIFE BUT CONTINUES IN A NEW REALM.

"We walk by faith" (2 Corinthians 5:7)

Jesus "appeared to the disciples as they walked on the Emmaus Road" (Mark 16:12). Jesus said, "I have gone before you to prepare a place for you". Jesus has gone to prepare a place for daddy and others. The flowers today represent, not only the love of family and friends but are symbolic of the resurrection garden. Jesus said, "Because I live, you will live also." Death and grave are not the end. They are the beginning of a new dimension of living. It is a birth from this life to the next life, from the material to the spiritual.

A small child asked his grandmother one day. "Nanny, what is it like to die?" His grandmother thought for a moment and then she said, "Death is when you leave your body. The real you is still alive but it leaves its physical body which will decay. You've seen a shell on a beach! That's when the fish or crab or whatever was in there left that shell. But it continues to live." We will lay down the physical body one day to take on a spiritual body. We are transformed to live an abundant life.

There is an old legend that says one day that Enoch was walking with God. They had walked until late in the day and the sun was setting. God said to Enoch, "The day is now late; we're closer to my house than yours, come stay with me. " Daddy had walked long down the road of life. He finally came to the place where God said to him, "We're now closer to my house than yours, "Come stay with me."

Daddy has placed his hand quietly in the hand of the Lord and has gone to dwell in the land that is fairer than day. I believe that he was met by his mother and father and other loving family members who preceded him in death. The fall colors around us symbolize leaves as they drop off the trees. It is a beautiful demise for the leaves. But we also know that in the springtime life will go on. My father's death is not the end of his life, but it is a springtime of a new beginning in the eternal realm, which God has prepared for all of us.

One of my favorite poets is John Greenleaf Whittier. Let me share these words from him.

Yet Love will dream, and Faith will trust,
(Since he who knows our need is just)
That somehow, somewhere, meet we must.
Alas for him who never sees

The stars shine through his cypress trees!
Who, hopeless, lays his dead away,
Nor looks to see the breaking day
Across the mournful marble play!
Who hath not learned, in hours of faith
The truth to flesh and sense unknown,
That life is ever Lord of Death,
And Love can never lose its own![18]

---

18 John Greenleaf Whittier, "Yet Love Will Dream," Morrison, *Masterpieces of Religious Verse*, 605

A HOMILY

FOR

MRS. ELSIE MAE SCOTT TUCK
(A BEAUTIFUL LADY)

JOHN 14:1-6

When Jesus wanted to use some images to describe his kingdom, He used images of the home, family, mother and father. Heavenly life was depicted as a home. He said that He had gone to prepare some rooms for us. Reflecting on mother's death ushers in many thoughts of home and family.

At the end of the worship service Sunday morning when I told our people that my mother had died, one of the ladies came up to me and said, "Your mother was a beautiful lady." I think that is true in many ways. I looked up the word *beautiful* in the dictionary and it says, "Beautiful is that which gives the highest degree of pleasure to the senses or to the mind; delights by inspiring affection or warm adoration; any very attractive feature." That image of Mother lingers in my mind.

REFLECTING ON THE PAST

In these few moments I want to share some of my memories of Mother. You have your memories and I have mine of Mother or NaNa. Mother was indeed a very attractive person physically. She took great pride in her youthful appearance. She loved for someone to say, when I or my sister or brother were with her, that she looked like our sister. She enjoyed that observation and seemed to take delight in it. And honestly it seemed true. She always looked very attractive and youthful. She was always stylish and well-groomed, with every hair in place. She liked beautiful clothes, furnishings for her home and jewelry. Pink, red, and lavender were among her favorite colors.

Mother did not have an easy childhood. Her father died when he was thirty-two. At the age of six, she and her two sisters were placed in the Miller Home where they lived until they finished school and later got married. I remember vividly the stories she shared from her experience in the home. Some of them were about hard times and the tough discipline that she received. I remember her telling about a minor accident she once had. The officials in the home cut her hair as punishment. At that time long hair was a sign of beauty. That seems like an unfair treatment. Yet, they did a lot of wonderful, good things for Mother and her sisters in the home.

One of the things I learned from my mother was that she was not defeated by hard times and difficulties. Hardships became a driving force. She did not fall apart. She did not have the help of a counselor or a psychiatrist. She lived through the depression and World War II. She was a survivor. She worked hard to make life good. She did not ask the question, "Why?" but "How and What do I need to do?" She did not expect others to do for her, but she sought to make her own way.

FAMILY TIME

She established and maintained a wonderful home and family. She and my father were married for sixty-four years. They were an example of endurance. They were not always easy to live with, as many of us are not. They were both strong, independent persons, as we know. Yet, later, they became dependent on and devoted to each other. They each loved and cared for one another. My mother took care of Daddy and waited on him. She used to talk about how he had been spoiled by his sisters, since he was the youngest of the children. Mother waited on him, and he wanted his meals only the way Elsie fixed them. Ham biscuits, butter beans, and corn pudding had to be fixed just like Elsie prepared them. Nobody else could do it like she could. I can remember when Daddy was getting ready for bed, he would say, "Elsie, unmake my bed." I don't know too many husbands whose wives "unmade" their bed for them. But, this was the special, loving relationship they had. We all know the loving care she gave Daddy while he was sick. She stood by him and waited upon him until he died.

Mother was both a homemaker and a working mom. When we were children, Mother was there at home with us. When we got into high school, she began to work as a store clerk at J. P. Bell's and Robertson's Drugs. She worked at Whitten's Funeral Home for awhile. After she retired, she worked at the sheltered workshop.

She got along marvelously well with the handicapped children. They loved her and she loved them. Mother liked people. She was gregarious. But she still prepared good, hot meals for her family every night, even when she worked. I read this quote from Maria Schell. "Knowing that you release your family in the morning into the day with your love and with your warmth is the richness of life." For Mother, this was true.

Mother was a hard-working person. I remember that she kept our home clean and spotless. She waxed the floors every Friday. The yard had to be manicured. She loved her roses and other flowers. For many years, we had vegetable gardens. She worked in those gardens and canned and froze what she got from the garden. That hard work was a part of her therapy. She also instilled in us the values of hard work, order, appreciation, discipline, independence, and the importance of family. My wife has never had to pick up a towel or clothing I dropped on the floor, because Mother made sure that I nor Preston or June would act like that. I knew that I would feel a spanking on my rear end any time when I did. Picking up after me has never been a problem for my wife.

Lessons Learned

Mother started us to church. We went clean and on time. We learned from mother something about how to exercise discipline. My brother and sister may disagree with this, but my mother used to say that I got more spankings than the both of them together. I don't know if that's true or not, but since I see my sister nodding, I guess it was true.

I remember one time, when we lived on Pocahontas Street, I went down into the woods. Although I was small, I wanted to start a fire. I did but the fire got away. Before I knew it, the whole woods was on fire. I remember running back up to the house when I heard the fire trucks coming. Mother said that I got into a little rocking chair and rocked back and forth. All she had to do was look at my face and see how white it was to know who started that fire. That was one of the few times I didn't get a spanking. But I still learned a great lesson from that experience.

Meal times were very important in our home. We always had a good, hot breakfast and supper. I saw on TV not long ago a talk about how every family ought to have at least one meal a week with your family. Well, we had several meals a day with our family, and Sunday dinner was the meal of the week. We learned early that we had to be on time for supper. We ate at 5:00 o'clock sharp. My brother, Preston, reminded me the other day about a fight I was engaged in up the street from our house. (I don't know if my church deacons ought to hear all of this). Because of the fight, I was late for supper. My mother sent Preston to get me and bring me home. But I wouldn't come. He stayed to watch the fight. He got a spanking and I got a spanking, too, because we were both late for supper. Mother expected us to be on time for meals no matter what.

Christmas was a celebrated and festive time in our lives. Our house was always brightly decorated with lights, colors and ornaments. There were many gifts and clothing. Mother was not a very expressive person in saying, "I love you." Rather than being verbal, she showed her love in other ways by providing for us a happy, wonderful time, especially at Christmas. The sights, sounds, smells and touches of Christmas will always live with me. We always came down the steps to the music of *Here Comes Santa Claus* playing on the record player. It was a happy, wonderful time. And I will always cherish the memories.

Our house was for many years a gathering place for us. Our families would gather, especially at holidays, for festive meals. I could still sleep in the same bed I slept in as a child. Now that chapter will end and we will sell the house where my parents lived for fifty years. That house will never again be the same place for us.

We also remember Mother's sense of humor. She loved a good story. She had a ringing laugh and good smile. She always had a way of embroidering on a tale. Her story seemed to grow bigger and bigger with each telling and grew a little different and bigger at other times. She loved children. She loved her grandchildren and great grandchildren. There are 10 grandchildren and 21 great-grandchildren. They were a vital part of her life. With all the grandchildren and great-grandchildren, she never forgot a birthday and got presents for everyone at Christmas.

Laura Woolley, the little girl next door, was probably eight years old when she wrote the following letter. She gave it to my mother when mother was about eighty-two. The poem-letter is entitled *My Best Older Friend* by Laura Woolley.

"My best older friend is Mrs. Tuck.
She is my neighbor.
Sometimes we talk together
I don't know how old she is
I think she is fifty-two
She plants bulbs most of the time She likes flowers.
I love her very much. She loves me too.
Sometimes I play in her basement. I hope she lives a long time."

JOURNEY'S END

Mother seemed to sense that the end was near. She spoke to friends and family that she was on the last lap. She had talked recently about Daddy having died three years ago. She acknowledged that she was getting weak and couldn't do much any more. She did not like to be dependent and not able to do her house and yard work.

We come to this moment, though, knowing that we are not alone. We come with family and friends and in the presence of God to sustain us. We have the comfort of God and our friends. The word "comfort" means "with strength." We face our grief not limited by our own strength, but we draw on the strength of God. Another woman going out of my church Sunday said to me, "The Lord is now going to take care of your mother. She is with God. We will take care of you." We have to take care of each other, knowing that there is strength from God.

Mother now begins her new journey from the physical life to the spiritual life. She will go to the spiritual realm to meet Daddy. And as a friend of mine said, "Her death was 'on time'." She lived to be eighty-five. It was a good life, a full life. She did not suffer for a long time. She lived in her own home. She was still alert to the end and died in her sleep.

A young boy, who was dying, asked his mother one day what it was like to die. She didn't know what to say at first and then she said to him, "Honey, do you remember when we would go down and visit grandmother. We would go on that long trip and sometimes you would fall asleep in her home. Your daddy and I would pick you up while you were asleep and place you in the car and then you would wake up the next morning in your own bed. Death is like that. You will go to sleep here in your physical bed and then you wake up in eternity in the bed God has prepared." Death is like that. We fall asleep here, and we wake up in the eternal room that God has prepared.

We have a copy of a birthday greeting card from her Sunday School with her picture on it which Mother received on her first birthday. Here is the greeting from her Cradle Roll Superintendent:

"What shall we ask for these little eyes?
Open them Lord.
To see in Thy Word Wondrous things.
Light them with love,
And shade them above with angels' wings."

Mother has indeed seen many wondrous things and even now sees more wondrous things. We affirm our faith today that death is not the end but the beginning. We lean in trust on the God of love. One of the great hymns is entitled *O Love That Wilt Not Let Me Go*.

O Love that wilt not let me go,
I rest my weary soul in thee;
I give thee back the life I owe,

That in thine ocean depths its flow
May richer, fuller be.

O Light that followest all my way,
I yield my flick'ring torch to thee;
My heart restores its borrowed ray,
That in they sunshine's glow its day
May brighter, fairer be.

O Joy that seekest me through pain,
I cannot close my heart to thee;
I trace the rainbow thro' the rain,
And feel the promise is not vain
That morn shall tearless be.

O Cross that liftest up my head,
I dare not ask to hide from thee;
I lay in dust life's glory dead,
And from the ground there blossoms red
Life that shall endless be.[19]

Loving Father, we thank you for the life of Elsie Tuck, NaNa, and her influence for good in our lives. We know we are the kind of persons we are and that we are richer because of her love and sacrifices. Comfort us with the assurance of Your peace and grace and with the knowledge of the eternal life she shares in Your endless love. Put the arms of Your love around us in the days ahead to accept our grief and live in the strength of Your abiding presence. In the name of Christ, we pray. Amen.

---

19 "O Love that Wilt Not Let Me Go," Hustad, *Hymns for the Living Church*, 351.

A Homily
for
Betty Mae Roll
(A Floral Decorator)

1 Corinthians 15:53-57
Romans 8:35-39

The Apostle Paul wrote in Ephesians 5:20 "Giving thanks always for all things." That is easy to do in good and pleasant times, but more difficult in hard and grieving times. But let's pause and see if we can find some ways even now to express our thanks to God even in the midst of our sadness.

We can pause now and thank God for the gift of the life of Betty Mae. She lived among us for seventy years but that was too brief. Even life at its longest can be too brief, especially for a loved one we have lost by death. We remember and reflect on her years of hopes, joys, blessings and service. We remember her years of service as a volunteer at the Virginia Baptist Hospital in discharge. At the gathering of friends at the reception last night at Tharp Funeral Home, I had several people speak of her dedicated work there. Several spoke about her faithful work on the church kitchen committee, with children at the church, with yard sales and other things. She was always unselfish and giving of herself and not asking anything in return. She also never met a stranger. One of the church members told me that when she first met him in the community, she invited him to her church. And he joined the church because of her friendship and invitation.

We can also thank God that flowers were a special focus of her beauty and creativity. Vickie reminded us that "Everything Betty Mae touched turned into something beautiful." She could pick up something at a junk yard, thrift shop, or a flea market and make it into a beautiful arrangement or special decoration. She had the gift to make something beautiful out of nothing. Think of all the churches where she did flowers for weddings and turned those special celebrative moments into beautiful lasting memories. Reflect on the beautiful Christmas decorations and arrangements she made, especially her special arrangements for the Stonegate Club House with the Nativity set as the central focus on the fireplace. She operated her own florist for thirty-five years, and taught floral design for twenty-five years. The words on the bottom of the Visitation brochure depict her gift, "Gone to the meadow to pick and arrange God's flowers."

We also thank God for her personal care of herself and that she was herself a beautiful person in appearance and spirit. As someone said, "She always looked liked she just stepped out of a band box. Her hair and make up were always in perfect place." She was always a caring, loving and unselfish person, who thought of others first. She was indeed feisty. She was also a person that you knew where she stood. She was plain spoken and you always knew what she thought. She also could be the life of the party. I had many persons express that to me last night at the funeral home. She was fun to be with and they spoke about how they would miss her ringing laughter. She was active in the Christian Woman's Club and the Sunset Garden Path and Richland Hills Garden Clubs. Her friends at the Garden Path Garden Club penned this note on the flowers they sent:

"She came to earth as a child of God and in her lifetime, with her creativity of beauty and love, gathered countless friends about her. Her sharing and caring ways were a wonderful example for all who were touched by her life. She has left footprints on many hearts as she traversed through her dash—1940—2011. Sadly now, for us, her circle of life is ended and one of earth's angels returns home, once again to be a child of God. We will miss her."

After moving to Stonegate, some of the ladies taught Betty Mae a card game called Hand and Foot, a form of Canasta. She had not played cards before and she loved it, often playing three or four times a week. Finally, her sickness blurred her vision and she finally had to quite because she was unable to focus. But until she reached that point her friends continued to come to her house so she could play.

Today we acknowledge the mystery of life and note that we all have questions about the "why" of cancer, heart attacks and other dread diseases or illnesses. There are no easy answers. **We can't understand all but we can still be thankful that we can affirm our trust in God and his goodness.** We know that death is a part of life as birth is. God is with us in both in our birth and in our death and our life in between. We are thankful that Betty Mae was able to face her cancer with courage and grace. During her three years of her battle with cancer she was uncomplaining and brave. She did not slow down but continued to play cards, do her volunteer and church work as long as she was able. She visited her granddaughter, Timbre, even when she herself did not feel like it. She prepared her own funeral by talking with her pastor several months in advance and selected her own flowers for the service.

No one could have been more loving and caring for her than Preston was through her long illness. They shared fifty-one years of married life together. He was there all the time of her illness and kept her at home and cared for her until the end. His love is an inspiration to us all. Both Vickie and Steve were also very attentive to their mother during this time of illness.

Today we can also thank God that death is not a wall but a door that opens from this material world into the spiritual world. Death is the end of her physical life but the beginning of a new life. Death is a birthing from this world into the spiritual presence of God. Betty's love of flowers can be a reminder to us that flowers today represent the resurrection garden. The spring flowers remind us of new life. And every bud on the flowers and trees reflect the promise of new life. Jesus said, "I have gone to prepare a place for you." Death is a birthing from this life to the life he has made ready for us. "For me to live is Christ," Paul writes, "and to die is to gain."

I heard about a small child that was dying and he asked his mother what it was like to die. She said, "Remember when you used to go visit your grandparents and fall asleep in their home in the bed there. And then later you would awaken the next day in your own bed here. Well, death is like falling asleep in your bed here and then awaking in your bed in heaven that God has prepared for you."

Today we affirmed that Betty Mae has move from the church mortal to the church immortal, from her material home to her spiritual home. One of our hymns reminds us:

O love that will not let me go,
I rest my weary soul in Thee;
I give Thee back the life I owe,
That in Thine ocean depths its flow
May richer, fuller be.[20]

*O loving Father, grant to Preston, Vickie and Steve your
strong presence in this their time of grief. Sustain them with
the assurance of the life everlasting Betty Mae shares with
You. We thank You for the years of her good life which she
lived among us. Give them comfort and peace in the days
ahead as they lean upon You and each other. Through Christ,
we pray. Amen.*

---

20   *Ibid.*

A Homily
for
Ruth Revell
(A Quilter)

"The Quilt of Life"

John 14:1-5, 27; John 20:24-28

A   t an exhibit of American quilts at the Oakland Art Museum, there was a beautiful quilt entitled, "Widow's Quilt." The artist had fashioned from her husband's clothes a tableau of their life together. She included scenes of their wedding day, the gravestone of a child among many others. Her pictures, meticulously veered and the uneven stitches were a powerful metaphor of her grief

Today we have gathered to see if we cannot capture a comforter of warmth and enduring beauty as we reflect on some patches of thought and stitches of memories about Ruth Revell. This will, of course, not be the whole story but a quick glance. We remember what beautiful sewing Ruth did, how she loved beautiful things and saw the wonderful possibilities in a piece of cloth. She was indeed a beautiful seamstress herself.

THE GOODNESS OF LIFE

One dimension in the quilt of Ruth's life would be an affirmation on the goodness of life itself We remember today, the good times and difficult times in Ruth's life. We remember the happy moment and sad times, victories and defeats, joys and sorrows, health and sickness, peace and struggles. We acknowledge that these are all a part of the fabric of life. Life comes to us as a wonderful gift. Ruth tried to live her life to the fullest. She did not blame God for her illness and suffering. She bore her illness with grace and dignity. These past few months have been a difficult time for Ruth. We can be thankful that her suffering and pain are over. God gives us the gift of life. What we make of this life is our gift to God. Ruth invested her life well.

THE LOVE OF GOD

Another dimension in the quilt of Ruth's life is an affirmation about the love of God. God's love comes to us as a great gift through creation and redemption. "God so loved ... that God gave." Ruth experienced this love of God, especially in church. Through her church she first learned about God's love and continued to grow in her faith. Ruth loved her church and was faithful in her attendance and support of it.

You could always see Ruth in her place on Sunday and Wednesday and at other special church functions. In the last few months, Ruth came to church when she did not feel like it. She even came not dressed in her very best, but sometimes dressed in a bathrobe and, brought by her sitter. But she felt this was the place she wanted to be. It was important for her to be in church and worship. Today, we acknowledge that Ruth knows God's love on a deeper, eternal level. She has now experienced a love which passes all understanding. "Thanks be to God for his inexpressible gift" (2 Corinthians 9:15).

GENEROSITY

Another panel in the quilt today is Ruth's generosity. Ruth had experienced God's blessings in a special way. She knew she was fortunate and blessed but she did no horde her possessions to herself but generously shared her good fortune with others. Ruth supported her church, special music and organ programs and mission causes. She was generous in her community and in her support of the University of North Carolina at Pembroke. An oriental rug hangs in the entranceway to the administrative building on the UNCP campus, her special gift to the university. Ruth also gave generously to the Boy's and Girl's Club, the Boys and Girls Home and many other causes that crossed racial and economic lines. She was generous to so many.

She took seriously her Lord's words, that "it is more blessed to give than to receive" (Acts 20:35). "Truly I say to you, as you do unto the least of these my brothers, you did it to me" (Matthew 25:40). She knew that giving was Christ-like, the most Christ-like thing that we can do. 1 Corinthians 13 tell us that love is a vital part of our living. This love is not abstract, but very personal, concrete, particular and specific. As she gave to help others, Ruth knew that she was giving to God. She has a great love for her fellow-man and wanted to assist all she could. Ruth did so much for so many. Her graciousness will be felt for years to come.

LIFE BEYOND DEATH

A final panel in this quilt is our affirmation in life beyond death. For the Christian, death is not the end. It is the doorway to a spiritual life. Jesus said, "Because I live, you will live also." He also said, "I have gone to prepare a place for you." He told us, "I am the resurrection and the life." Death is a passageway from this life to the next life. It is not a dead-end but a birthing from this life to the next, from the physical world into the eternal world. Ruth has now joined her husband in the land that is fairer than day. He died in 1976 and they are now reunited in God's wonderful home. Ruth trusted God and put her hand in God's hand. In quiet faith, she leaned back and trusted God during the time of her illness. Just as a small child in a dark room reaches out to hold the hand of his mother or father in that moment of darkness, so we know today that Ruth has reached out her hand in the dark valley and grasped the hand of Jesus our Lord who has carried her through the valley into life eternal.

We know that Ruth's good influence will continue. The season of her influence will not be concluded with her death. She is no longer with us and the joy and happiness she left will be missed. Nevertheless, she will be long remembered. The impact of her smile, generosity, service, love and devotion will continue to be felt after she has gone. Her influence for good, joy and radiance will leave an afterglow among us. Life will be different without her. Her influence will still be felt.

Just as Jesus assured Mary at the grave of Lazarus that he was the resurrection and the life, today we trust that same Christ in faith and affirm that death is a birthing from this life to the life beyond. We affirm with the apostle Paul, "what is sown is perishable, what is raised is imperishable. It is sown in dishonor but it is raised in glory. It is sown a physical body; it is raised a spiritual body. Death is swallowed up in victory. Thanks be to God who gives us the victory through our Lord, Jesus Christ."

Calmly and quietly, today we note the home-going of this good woman-Ruth Revell. May God give you the strength and comfort of his spirit to guide you as you face the future.

Loving God, bind up the broken hearts today with the balm of your presence. Draw all the family members and friends close to yourself and may they sense your shepherding care and presence in the days ahead. May the memories of the good life with the assurance of life everlasting give to each of us in this hour comfort and assurance.

24.

A HOMILY

FOR

DR. NORMAN GEORGE
(A VETERINARIAN)

GENESIS 6:13-22

On the bookshelf in my study is a carved set of Noah's Ark. This was a gift given to me by my daughter. It has the ark with Noah standing by and all the animals being led on board. As I looked at that ark last night, I thought that Dr. George is a type of Noah. He was always seeking to bring animals into the ark of comfort, health, security, freedom from pain and to give them love. Let us pause now to reflect on this modern day Noah who was without question, a first class veterinarian.

A DEDICATED WORKER

Like Noah, Dr. George was a dedicated worker. Over sixty years ago, Dr. George became the county's first full time veterinarian. He was the oldest practicing veterinarian in North Carolina. In his early years of practice, when people could not pay, some would pay him in eggs, or butter or with whatever they could. He did not charge a lot, but he sought to take care of the needs as he saw them. Dr. George loved his work with animals. He was asked when he went to the hospital once, if he had any hobbies. "Work," he said, "is my hobby. I enjoy what I do." Dr. George helped train most of the veterinarians in this area. He helped some get through school when the going got tough or the studying became hard. He even would spend some time tutoring them.

When others in our community had difficult problems with drugs or other things, Dr. George reached out to help them. He helped get them back on the right track. He was a caring, concerned man, who sought to help all in need. On November 18th, 1989, the mayor issued a proclamation declaring that day as Norman George Day in honor and appreciation for Dr. George's work in our community. Up until the end, Dr. George was continuing to do research and stay on top of his field. He always wanted to be informed and to do the very best work he could. He was without question, a dedicated man.

A MAN OF COMPASSION

Like Noah, Dr. George was a man of compassion. Dr. George deeply loved animals and people. He worked on all kinds of animals, large and small. He worked on mules, cows, horses, dogs and cats and even circus animals. People can recall seeing him working on camels. He worked on pets or service animals. He was physically strong, himself and often had to lift or move some of these animals. Wherever there was a need, Dr. George would go. Carol was chastising him once because he went out to assist a sick cow late one night. "How did you get there?" she asked him because she knew that he couldn't drive then. "They came and got me," he replied. Just think, Dr. George was in his eighties then.

Like our Lord and Master, Dr. George showed compassion to animals and to the owners of these animals. He followed our Lord's example, easing pain, hurt, suffering and disease in animals. He always remembered the names of his customers. He would draw on the best resources he could. He sometimes used the equipment and knowledge of surgeons, radiologists, pathologists and others. He wanted to do the best he could to alleviate pain and suffering. Dr. George was also a strong supporter and advocate for the Agricultural Center which he helped bring to our community.

John Greenleaf Whittier has a poem entitled "The Healer." This poem expresses appreciation for the work of someone like Dr. George.

> So stood of old the holy Christ Amidst the suffering throng
> With whom His lightest touch sufficed
> To make the weakest strong.
> That healing gift He lends to them
> Who use it in His name;
> The power that filled His garment's hem
> Is evermore the same.
>
> The paths of pain are thine.

Go forth with patience, trust, and hope;
The sufferings of a sin-sick earth
Shall give thee ample scope.

Beside the unveiled mysteries
Of life and death go stand,
With guarded lips and reverent eyes
And pure of heart and hand.

So shalt thou be with power endued
From Him who went about
Thy Syrian hillsides doing good,
And casting demons out.

That Good Physician liveth yet
Thy friend and guide to be;
The Healer by Gennesaret
Shall walk the rounds with thee.[21]

Dr. George was the beloved physician of animals in our community. We can be thankful that he lived among us.

A Strong Faith

Like Noah, Dr. George had a strong faith. This reserved, quiet, scholarly, compassionate man also had a deep faith. He always began his day with scripture and prayer. It was said that he could pray a very moving, beautiful, prayer. He continued this devotional practice up until the very end of his life. Like Noah, he trusted God. He did not understand all of the things that had happened to him. But in quiet faith and trust, he leaned back on God.

Today, we affirm that death is not the end. But it is the beginning of a new life. It is a birth from the physical life to the spiritual life. Dr. George has gone now to be in that spiritual realm. We

---

21 John Greenleaf Whittier, "The Healer," Morrison, *Masterpieces of Religious Verse*, 420.

trust the words of our Lord when He said, "I have gone to prepare a place for you." Jesus also told us, "I am the resurrection and the life." Jesus reminded us, "Let not your heart be troubled." We affirm today that Dr. George's suffering is over. He is in the land that is free of pain and sorrow.

No one could have issued more love and care for him than Kate and other family members had done. We know that life will be different without him. Dr. George's influence in our community has touched the lives of so many and will continue to do so for years to come. A family member said that when he died there was a peaceful look on his face, but one small tear they noticed on his cheek. Maybe this was his regret in leaving his family and friends. But he also knew now that he had entered that celestial bliss.

One of my favorite theologians is Scottish teacher, John Baillie. He tells a story of a physician going to visit a church member who was ill and dying. The man was frightened of death and he spoke to him about his fear. The doctor heard a scratching at the door, as they were talking. He said to the man, "Do you hear that scratching at the door? That's my dog. He has followed me here. He has never been here in your house before, but he knows that his master is here and he believes that wherever his master is it is okay. He wants to be with him. Soon you will die but you will go to be with the Master, and we know that everything will be fine." Today, we know that Dr. George has gone to be with the Master. We trust God and lean back in quiet confidence affirming the life everlasting that he has in Christ Jesus, our Lord.

> *Healing Lord, we thank you for the life of this good man, Dr. Norman George. We thank you for his impact in our community, his influence for good among family and friends. We pray that you will put the arms of your love around this family today and draw them close unto yourself. May they sense your compassionate love. Now may your comfort, peace and love watch over and bless them now and forevermore. Amen.*

A Homily

for

Copeland Howard Shaw, Sr.
(A Beach Lover)

"The Waves of Life"

Psalm 42:7-8

Copeland loved the beach. The beach helped him release his stress as he would sit in his rocking chair on his front porch at Holden Beach. He enjoyed listening to and watching the waves break on the shore at Holden each. It was relaxing for him. When we watch and listen to the waves, they can remind us of many things. Let us see if they cannot offer us some help in our time of grief

WAVES OF REASSURANCE

We are not alone in our suffering and pain. Remember that Christ is present. I believe that Copeland knew that. He drew upon the presence of Christ in the midst of his suffering and pain. The family can do that today. Remember that Jesus said, "I am with you always." The apostle Paul reminds us that, "Nothing separates us from the love of God." Today, lean upon the reassurance of God's presence with you in your grief Let the waves of God's reassuring presence warm and strengthen you.

WAVES OF RECOLLECTION

Today we pause to remember how Copeland honored his own parents. He put his own family first. He was always a hard-working man. He and Peter founded the Business Linen Supply Company. Later, he purchased Peter's part of the business. Copeland sold the business four or five years ago. Copeland loved to say, "I take in washing for a living." Copeland was also in the Navy and served in Korea.

Copeland loved his family. He taught them to work hard because he found that nothing comes easily in life. He reminded them that, "if all else fails, you have your family. Family is there when you need them." He reminded them that when you put your mind to a task, keep trying and keep your heart and faith right. Copeland loved his children, Rusty and Susan, and the grandchildren, Jamie and Jennifer. He was a devoted family man. He was a giving person to them. He often liked to joke with his grandchildren. During the last few years, he watched the Super Bowl game with the grandchildren. That was a special time he had with them.

When James was young, Copeland used to help him make model airplanes. He also taught James how to play the trumpet. He built a tree house for James and Jenny and earlier he gave Jennifer a North Carolina State Puppet. He was a big State fan. He took his children to church on Wednesday night as long as he was able. He taught them respect, to work hard and many other things. He reminded them not to do half of a job but the whole thing.

WAVES OF COMFORT

The word, "comfort," comes from two Latin words, "*con*" and "*fortis*," which mean "with strength." We know that we cannot bear this grief in our own strength. We need the comfort and strength of God. So, today the family leans upon God for comfort and support. We know that it is okay to cry. Life will be different without Copeland. The family today, can be comforted by God's love. The arms of Christ are around you. Feel the comforting presence of His grace and strength.

WAVES OF GRATITUDE

Waves of gratitude come washing over us as we reflect on Copeland's life. He was a good man who lived a full life. Today we can remember the good and difficult times, the happy and sad times, and still be grateful for his love and support. We are thankful that God has been present with us and Copeland in all things, during times of sickness and in health, when Copeland was strong, and also when he was weak. We can be thankful for his good influence upon us and we can also be thankful that his suffering is now over.

WAVES OF GOD'S PEACE

Jesus said, "My peace I give to you." Today we can claim the peace of Jesus Christ within. We have the inner calm that comes from the presence of Christ. Although we may be surrounded by the storms of grief all around us, when we have God within, we know we can face whatever comes. The calm of Christ at the center of our lives is like the peace at the center of a hurricane. No matter what is going on around us, there is that inner peace.

The last time I visited Copeland, I prayed for him as I did each time. His custom was to hold my hand. I reached out and took his and when I had finished praying, and got ready to release my hand from his, he continued to hold onto my hand. Then he prayed for me. He thanked me for my support and attention to his family through the years and indicated that he would miss me when I left. His prayer for me gave me that sense of his own inner peace and showed that he felt comfortable enough to reach and pray for me as his pastor as well as receive a prayer. This was the only time that I ever remember him doing that.

WAVES THAT TAKE US INTO ETERNAL LIFE

There is the final wave that comes over us and takes us on the journey into eternal life. We cross uncharted waters to go into the presence of God. We travel on a pathway that no one in this life has until death claims us. Walt Whitman has a poem entitled, "The Sea of Faith." Listen to his words of assurance,

Passage, immediate passage!
The blood burns in my veins!
Away, O soul! Hoist instantly the anchor!
Cut the hawsers- haul out- shake out every sail!
Have we not stood here like trees in the ground long
enough?
Have we not groveled here long enough, eating and drink-
ing like mere brutes?
Have we not darkened and dazed ourselves with books long
enough?
Sail forth- steer for the deep water only,
Reckless, 0 soul, exploring, I with thee and thou with me,
For we are bound whither mariner has not yet dared to go,

And we will risk the ship ourselves and all.
O my brave soul!
O farther, farther sail!
O daring joy, but safe! Are they not all the seas of God?
O farther, farther sail![22]

These words assure us that we can steer forward, we can steer out into the deep waters and be assured that the deep waters themselves are the seas of God. No matter where we travel we are assured that God goes before us to sustain us. Death for the Christian is not the end but a new beginning. It is a doorway to a new way of life. We walk through the valley of the shadow of death with the presence of Christ. Death is a birthing from this life to the life eternal. We place our hands in the Father's hand, assured of His support and guidance. Jesus has promised, "I will not leave you comfortless. I have gone to prepare a place for you." Today we rest in the assurance of the presence of Christ and in the strength of His grace. We know that Copeland has gone on to be with the God that he loved and we trust God and lean fully on God's grace.

Eternal Father, we thank you again for the life of Copeland Shaw. We pray that you will surround Sue, Randy, James and Jenny and other family members with your love. We are thankful that his suffering is over and he has gone to be with you. Now we pray that your comfort, love and strength, will surround this family both now and forevermore. Amen.

---

22 Walt Whitman, "Passage to India," *Leaves of Grass*, vol. II (New York: G. P. Putman's Sons, 1903), 193-194.

A Homily

for

David A. Jones
(A Christmas Eve Funeral)

Luke 2:10

"Behold I bring you good news of great joy for unto you is born this day a Savior who is Christ the Lord."

As we come before this moment of grief, we acknowledge that for many this is a happy, joyous time because it is Christmas. For us, it is a sad time because death has come into our lives at this normally happy time. But let us allow the message of this Christmas season to speak to us in this moment. Surely, there is a message of good news that can speak to us in the midst of our sadness.

CHRISTMAS CAUSES US TO PAUSE AND REFLECT.

At Christmastime we slow down and think more about family and friends and the love we share. So on this Christmas Eve we pause now and reflect on the life of David A. Jones. We know that he loved this community and thought Robeson County the best place in the world. He said once, "The air always smelled better on Barker Ten Mile Road than any place else." He loved his farm and enjoyed planning and working on it. He liked to talk about his twenty-two goats and how they were growing. He told me once that he was going to let me borrow one of his goats to eat up my weeds, including the poison ivy that I had growing. Friends and family knew of his love for goats and gave him small, model goats.

Family members said that he was their best friend. He was a wonderful father, was a strong, loving, devoted man. He loved Pat and they shared forty-eight years together. He was a good father and a wonderful grandfather. He was the father of three daughters and three grandchildren. David loved this community and was a successful business man. He started his automobile dealership in Fairmont and then later moved to Lumberton as owner of the Buick-Cadillac Dealership. In an article in the *Robesonian* in which there was a picture where David received a twenty-fifth anniversary award, he credited Pat with encouraging him to expand his business to the full extent that he had hoped to accomplish. David started with nothing and became a successful businessman. David was a planner. He planned what he wanted to do and stuck to it. He would not be swayed from his goal.

This was true with his life. He planned and stuck by that goal. He loved cars and was proud of his business. He put his family first and he jokingly, but sincerely, said to a friend once that he was going to marry Patsy even before she knew it. His family came first to him. He was a good husband and a good citizen.

People always knew where David stood. He word was his bond. He was a person who said what he thought. Happy Lewis said of David once, "He was right down the middle of the road. If he promised, he would do it." He was good to his friends. He loved people and liked to talk to them. David enjoyed the Men's Fellowship Class at First Baptist Church. He had many good friends there who supported and encouraged him, especially during his time of illness. He was also a 32nd Degree Mason and a Shriner. David said that he saw many changes in his life and community. He liked to talk about these changes as he remembered them. Today we remember this good man and the life he lived and the lives that he has touched.

THE CHRISTMAS SEASON REMINDS US OF THE EMMANUEL - GOD'S PROMISE - "GOD WITH US."

God is now with you in the midst of your grief. You are not alone. You do not bear that grief by yourself. You have family, friends, your church and the community. But most importantly you know that God is present with you. That is the wonderful promise of Christmas. We never have to bear any load completely alone. The one who is the Good Shepherd, the Emmanuel, is there with you. Remember then, drawing on David's love for goats, that Christ is the Good Shepherd. The Good Shepherd is there with you to support you in your grief. The Lord is our Shepherd and we know that He will continue to support us.

We also know that no one could have been more loving and caring for David during his illness than Patsy and other family members. They reached out to him and gave him support, love and attention during his time of illness. No one could have asked for more than what they gave him during this time.

Ann Weems has written a Christmas poem that reminds us that God is present with us on the darkest of days.

INTO THIS SILENT NIGHT

Into this silent night
as we make our weary way we know not where,
just when the night becomes its darkest and we cannot see
our path,
just then
is when the angels rush in,
their hands full of stars.[23]

Remember that God is there with you on the darkest of the days. God is there with you in your grief. God will bear you up and give you strength. He will give you light in the midst of your darkness. Be encouraged by knowing that God is present.

CHRISTMAS IS GOOD NEWS IN THE MIDST OF BAD NEWS.

Mary and Joseph had a difficult time according to the Christmas story. They had to make a difficult journey to Bethlehem when Mary was expecting a child. Herod was seeking the child to put him to death. Israel was in slavery to the Roman Empire during this time. But in the midst of all of this great sadness, difficulty and bad news, God came with the wonderful Good News of the Incarnation.

In the midst of your grief there comes good news. Death is not the end. There is a birth from this world to the next. Death opens the door here into the spiritual realm. Jesus said, "Because I live, you shall live also." "I have come that you might have life and have it more abundantly." David has gone now to join his brother Bill who also died this year on July 4th. We know that one day we will all pass through that doorway to the life beyond. But we have the assurance that this life is not the end but that life goes on in

---

23 Ann Weems, *Kneeling in Bethlehem*, 52.

the eternal realm. One of my favorite hymns at Christmastime was written by Phillips Brooks. He penned these words:

> How silently, how silently
> The wondrous gift is giv'n!
> So God imparts to human hearts
> The blessings of His heav'n.
>
> No ear may hear His coming,
> But in this world of sin,
> Where meek Souls will receive Him still
> The dear Christ enters in.[24]

Listen in the midst of your sorrow to hear the angelic voices - the voice of God. God comes on the darkest of days to let us know that he is present. On this Christmas Eve in the midst of your grief, remember that we celebrate the birth of the Immanuel. God is with you to strengthen you, encourage you and sustain you. May you sense God's love and grace.

> *Ever Blessing Lord, we thank you for the life of this good man, David Jones. We pray now that you will surround this family with the arms of your love. May the embrace of your presence today and in the days to come give them assurance. Give them an awareness today of the life everlasting that we share through Jesus Christ. May the comfort of Your presence abide with them both now and always. Amen.*

---

24 Phillips Brooks, "O Little Town of Bethlehem," Hustad, *Hymns for the Living Church*, 121.

If I had had this book when I was a seminary student (also many years ago) I would have been a far better preacher than I was. I highly recommend it to others!

John Killinger

Former Professor of Preaching at Vanderbilt Divinity School and Princeton

In these sermons I found the good news of Jesus presented in a fresh, realistic, warm, encouraging, and interesting way.

Fisher Humphreys

Professor of Divinity *Emeritus* Samford University

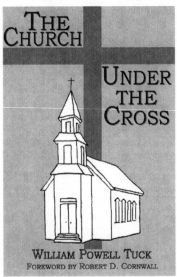

MORE FROM ENERGION PUBLICATIONS

Personal Study

Holy Smoke! Unholy Fire	Bob McKibben	$14.99
The Jesus Paradigm	David Alan Black	$17.99
When People Speak for God	Henry Neufeld	$17.99
The Sacred Journey	Chris Surber	$11.99

Christian Living

It's All Greek to Me	David Alan Black	$3.99
Grief: Finding the Candle of Light	Jody Neufeld	$8.99
My Life Story	Becky Lynn Black	$14.99
Crossing the Street	Robert LaRochelle	$16.99
Life as Pilgrimage	David Moffett-Moore	14.99

Bible Study

Learning and Living Scripture	Lentz/Neufeld	$12.99
From Inspiration to Understanding	Edward W. H. Vick	$24.99
Philippians: A Participatory Study Guide	Bruce Epperly	$9.99
Ephesians: A Participatory Study Guide	Robert D. Cornwall	$9.99
Ecclesiastes: A Participatory Study Guide	Russell Meek	$9.99

Theology

Creation in Scripture	Herold Weiss	$12.99
Creation: the Christian Doctrine	Edward W. H. Vick	$12.99
The Politics of Witness	Allan R. Bevere	$9.99
Ultimate Allegiance	Robert D. Cornwall	$9.99
History and Christian Faith	Edward W. H. Vick	$9.99
The Journey to the Undiscovered Country	William Powell Tuck	$9.99
Process Theology	Bruce G. Epperly	$4.99

Ministry

Clergy Table Talk	Kent Ira Groff	$9.99
Overcoming Sermon Block	William Powell Tuck	$12.99
Holidays, Holy Days, and Special Days	William Powell Tuck	$16.99

Generous Quantity Discounts Available
Dealer Inquiries Welcome
Energion Publications — P.O. Box 841
Gonzalez, FL 32560
Website: http://energionpubs.com
Phone: (850) 525-3916

CPSIA information can be obtained at www.ICGtesting.com
Printed in the USA
LVOW08s2312190816

501071LV00001B/8/P